The Good University

About the author

Raewyn Connell is Professor Emerita at the University of Sydney, a life member of NTEU, and one of Australia's leading social scientists. Her writing is widely cited and has been translated into nineteen languages. Recent books are *Southern Theory* (2007); *Gender: In World Perspective* (with Rebecca Pearse, 2015); *El género en serio* (2015); and *Knowledge & Global Power* (with Fran Collyer, João Maia and Robert Morrell, 2019). Raewyn is a long-term participant in the labour and peace movements.

The Good University

What universities actually do and why it's time for radical change

Raewyn Connell

The Good University: What Universities Actually Do and Why It's Time for Radical Change was first published in 2019 by Zed Books Ltd, The Foundry, 17 Oval Way, London SE11 5RR, UK. www.zedbooks.net. This edition is published by Monash University Publishing, by arrangement with Zed Books Ltd.

Monash University Publishing
Matheson Library and Information Services Building
40 Exhibion Walk
Monash University
Clayton, Victoria, 3800, Australia
www.publishing.monash.edu
www.publishing.monash.edu/books/gu-9781925835038.html

Typeset in Akzidenz Grotesk and Haarlemmer
by Swales & Willis Ltd, Exeter, Devon, UK
Index by Kath Selkirk
Cover design by Les Thomas
Series: Education

A catalogue record for this book is available from the National Library of Australia

Printed in Australia by Griffin Press an Accredited ISO AS/NZS 14001:2004 Environmental Management System printer.

ISBN 9781925835038 pb
ISBN 9781925835045 pdf
ISBN 9781925835052 epub

Contents

Introduction

This book is about universities: their work and workers, their colourful history and current troubles – and above all, how we can get good universities for the future. I have wrestled with these questions for a long time, as many have done; but a specific event persuaded me to write this book.

In 2013 a long industrial dispute broke out at the University of Sydney, where I worked. Early in the year, management proposed a real wage cut over time, and a string of changes that worsened conditions of employment, including removing academic freedom from the agreement. Union members voted to strike, and long months of inch-by-inch bargaining followed, punctuated by days on picket. There was inventive cultural struggle, with videos made by striking workers, Open Letters on the internet, a light-hearted demonstration with union balloons at the Open Day, a satirical yoga display of 'flexibility', and more. I was in the room on Tuesday 1 October when a packed meeting of academic and operations staff voted, after sharp debate, to accept the wages-and-conditions deal that had finally been negotiated between the union and the management.

In 2013 the union did well. But it was obvious that for many years university workers have been on the defensive, not only against management but also against government and corporate power. Standing on the picket line I felt we needed bolder agendas for the knowledge institutions we *should* be building. We launched a discussion of this issue during the strike, and I continue it here.

There's an angry, sometimes anguished, debate inside universities. Critics speak of outdated pedagogy, exploitation of young staff, distorted and even faked research, outrageous fees, outrageous pay for top managers, corporate rip-offs, corruption, sexism, racism, and mickey-mouse degrees. For a couple of decades we have been hearing laments about *The University in Ruins*, *The Universities in Crisis*, and *The Fall of the Faculty*. There is criticism from outside the university world, too. While I was writing this book, the government of the United States was taken over by a right-wing group contemptuous of university-educated 'elites' and university-based science.[1]

Many other governments have been squeezing funds to universities. In 2010 the Tory-dominated government of Britain announced a plan to chop out all public funding for most undergraduate degrees, forcing students to pay the deficit. The scheme was presented, with startling hypocrisy, as 'empowering' students via market choice. Student fees have risen in most countries. The resulting debt has become a monster. At the end of 2016, total student debt in the United States stood at $1.31 *trillion*, having increased by $31 billion in the year.[2]

There is rising distrust between university workers and university managements, as the events at Sydney show. There are also tensions between students and staff. In South Africa the University of Cape Town was massively disrupted in 2015 by the 'Rhodes Must Fall' movement, led by Black students, and a national protest movement about fees followed. There are tensions among students and between students and managers. In India the University of Hyderabad was convulsed in 2015–16 by conflict between caste-based student groups, inept management and heavy-handed intervention by the Hindu-nationalist government.

And yet, higher education is booming. According to United Nations figures, in 1970 only about 10 per cent of the relevant age-group, worldwide, had gone to a university or college. By 2015 the proportion had more than tripled, to about 36 per cent. The official figures for 2015 showed more than 200 million higher education students enrolled, worldwide. Simon Marginson, a noted analyst of the political economy of universities, observes that many countries are now approaching a high-participation system where more than half the relevant age-group go into higher education.[3]

To hear the official voices of university managers, it is all going brilliantly. If you look up almost any university on the Web, you will be shown pictures of fine clean buildings, gleaming laboratories, contented staff, wise chancellors, extremely green lawns and deliriously happy students.

If you read the public thoughts of university leaders you get a similar picture. Professor Derek Bok, the former President of Harvard University (number one in the global league tables), is regarded as an intellectual leader in higher education, something of a liberal reformer who in 2003 warned against 'excesses' of commercialization. Ten years later he published a big book called *Higher Education in America* that presented the US system as the wonder of the world. At the end of this survey Bok could see only two urgent problems: getting even more young Americans into college; and sprucing up their courses while getting them to put more sweat into studying.

In 2010 Professor Glyn Davis, Vice-Chancellor of the University of Melbourne (number one in the local league tables) published *The Republic of Learning*, based on a series of radio talks. This is a relentlessly cheerful account of Australian university life that out-Boks Bok in complacency. 'We have in our midst an array of institutions committed to higher education, filled with great minds, devoted to teaching, engagement and research', Davis concluded. Nothing could possibly be wrong that a bit more money won't fix.[4]

University presidents, vice-chancellors and rectors do have something to be cheerful about. Their own salary packages, in large, profitable or prestigious universities in the richer countries, now run at a million dollars a year, with the fattest cat – at Wilmington University in the United States – collecting $5.4 million a year. That doesn't put them among the billionaires, but it certainly puts them in the One Per Cent, the ruling class of international capitalism. They have suits, language and attitudes to match. There is a truly startling economic gap between the top-level managers and the mass of precarious, outsourced, part-time and adjunct workers who actually make their universities work. It is not surprising there is distrust and tension.[5]

What exactly is a university? Technically, it is any institution with the legal power to grant degrees, or equivalent qualifications – bachelor's and master's degrees, doctorates and licenciates. This power was highly restricted in the days when founding a university needed a Charter from a pope, king or emperor, or a separate Act of Parliament. A strong rationale was required for any new foundation. There were twenty years of debate before the colonial University of Sydney opened in the 1850s; and sharp debates in the 1960s about the founding of the Open University in Britain and Jawaharlal Nehru University in India. Now the power to grant degrees has become much easier to get. Neoliberal governments have devised laws under which entrepreneurs can set up teaching institutions, call them universities, and simply have them registered administratively. That smoothed the path for a surge of privately owned universities, one of the big changes globally in the last three decades.[6]

The public/private division is only the beginning of diversity. In a recent article G. D. Sharma lists the different kinds of universities that are found in India today. They are: national and state-level public universities; for-profit private universities, of greatly varying size and quality; unitary vs affiliating universities (I will explain these terms shortly); residential vs non-residential universities; specialized universities in different parts of the country for agriculture, engineering, medicine and law; some universities based on indigenous knowledges; open universities, including the very large Indira Gandhi Open University established in 1985; and a stack of management and technology institutes, some of which are 'deemed-to-be universities' (an official term) and are entitled to grant degrees. Beyond all these, India has a huge range of local colleges that give diplomas and certificates. And that is all in one country – making, in student numbers, one of the three biggest higher education systems in the world.[7]

So much diversity makes the head spin. Is it sensible to talk about 'the university' – even in ruins – any more? Is it credible to put all these institutions on a single scale in a league table? The size and complication of the global higher education sector, and the multiple purposes that universities serve, are confronting.

And yet ... The name is not empty, and the power to grant degrees is not just a formality. It has economic and social consequences for the student, for the institution and for the government. There are reasons why all these parties *want* something defined as a university. I am reminded of Italo Calvino's novel *Invisible Cities*, where the traveller Marco Polo reports to the emperor Kublai Khan about the fabulous diversity of cities he has visited. They are cities of the desert and the coast, cities of the dead, upside-down cities, and so on. As the conversations go on, the traveller and the emperor begin to realize that all are, in some sense, the same city.

There is no deep purple essence of a university, able to be celebrated or betrayed. However there is a great deal of overlap in what different universities and their workers actually *do*; and that common ground is the subject-matter of this book.

What universities are supposed to do is teaching and research. That is the conventional view, and there is truth in it, though not the whole truth. The combination is historically recent. Early-modern European universities did little research; their curriculum was based on traditional texts, written centuries earlier by saints, philosophers and lawyers. The scientific revolution occurred mostly outside the universities. As recently as the mid-nineteenth century a famous tract, John Henry Newman's *The Idea of a University*, argued that a good university should do no research at all! Its proper job was to broaden the minds of young gentlemen by exposing them to the classics.[8]

But Newman's idea of a university was already obsolete. In the early nineteenth century new models of higher education emerged in three powerful European states. In republican and Napoleonic France, specialized centres of professional education were created, entered only by rigorous examination. They included the famous *École polytechnique* and the *École normale supérieure*. In monarchical Hannover and Prussia, the Universities of Göttingen and Berlin pioneered a model of free intellectual enquiry, with collegiality between professors and students. The role of the university was to wrestle with problems whose answers were *not* known, rather than to expound traditional knowledge.

In England, the University of London was set up to affiliate existing colleges through an examination system. This allowed expansion more easily than the single-campus unitary model. By the simple move of allowing outside students to sit for the exams, a mechanism for distance education was born. The University of London became the centre of an astonishing spiderweb of study centres; by the 1940s it had more than 50 overseas centres. Distance education fed into the television-and-radio work of Open Universities. They in turn led to the MOOCs (massive open online courses) of the twenty-first century.[9]

The European reforms were pushed farther in the enormous economic boom of the late nineteenth century in the United States. Old colonial universities like Harvard were re-jigged as research centres, new universities with graduate schools were set up (e.g. Johns Hopkins, and the Rockefeller-financed University of Chicago), and public higher education expanded. Disciplinary societies such as the American Economic Association were founded. In the Gilded Age of industrial capitalism, a powerful institutional base was created for a vision of knowledge as a compact array of secular, research-based, professionalized disciplines. This is still the dominant model of organized knowledge in the university world.[10]

Most universities today do more teaching than researching. A good many do only teaching, including for-profit private universities. There have been systems where research and teaching were separated by design. In the Soviet Union, independent India and early communist China, the research effort was concentrated in elite academies and institutes distinct from the university system. But some connection was necessary – or, as critics pointed out, where would the next generation of researchers come from?

So the Göttingen/Berlin ideal of a synthesis of research and teaching survived. It was taken for granted in the recent Chinese attempt to create 'world-class universities' by pouring a river of gold into a small elite group, through the central government's Project 985 launched in 1998. The universities at the dizzy heights of the global league tables all combine teaching and research: Harvard, Stanford, Berkeley, Cambridge, MIT, the Sorbonne. So does the Humboldt-Universität zu Berlin, as it is now called, which records among its past students Karl Marx and Otto von Bismarck and among its professors Georg Hegel and Albert Einstein.

The modern teaching-and-research university has, in a sense, conquered the world. But as university systems have grown to their current size, their problems have also grown and toxic effects have been more painfully felt. The strikes and occupations, and the talk of universities in crisis, are not in contradiction with the signs of success. The prosperity and the problems are deeply linked.

Do we need universities at all? It is a question worth thinking about. There are other ways to organize research, to do teaching and learning, and to spread knowledge in the age of the internet. I will discuss some in the final chapters of the book. But universities as institutions are where we have to start in thinking about organized knowledge and higher education today, so they will be the focus of my argument.

Universities represent, collectively, a tremendous social asset, produced by the effort of many thousands of workers and students over long periods of time. Universities educate the professions on which public health, public education, modern communications and social services rely. They produce most of the technical knowledge that goes into economic change (think information sciences, molecular biology, nanotechnology, solar energy). They are the source, directly or indirectly, of much of the critical thinking and imagination in culture and politics.

But that social asset can be used for different purposes. It can be made a tool of power: that is how we got atomic weapons. It has historically been used to exclude many groups: women, colonized peoples, working classes, Catholics, Dalits, Jews, Protestants, and others. In our time, universities are increasingly under the control of hard-faced business elites. Degrees can be used as gateways to networks and social privilege. The marketing slogans recently used by Australian universities include 'Your Advantage', 'Worldly', and 'Own the Future'. If we want a democratic society in our future, we must find a better logic than that.[11]

The Good University is a search for this better logic. It is easy to produce a wish list of reforms. The exercise can be useful, if only to challenge the numbing official propaganda about 'excellence', 'competition' and 'achievement'. But we need more than wish lists to make convincing strategies of change. We have to dig into the basic make-up of the institution and its conditions of existence.[12]

My argument has three main steps. We cannot understand research or teaching without recognizing them as forms of work. We need to explore the labour that produces organized knowledge, and the way research work generates truth (Chapter 1). We need to understand the work of teaching and learning at the advanced levels that universities are supposed to reach (Chapter 2). And to understand universities at work we must consider their workforce, and the cooperation that makes their work effective (Chapter 3).

My argument then moves to a larger scale. The research-based knowledge formation has always been part of a *global* economy of knowledge, and we need to understand the worldwide relationships and hierarchies involved (Chapter 4). Universities are funded, and criticized, because of their social and economic effects. We need to examine how they create privilege, and how that effect can be challenged (Chapter 5). Both globally and locally, universities have been swept up in the triumph of the neoliberal market agenda. We need to understand the new managerialism and its effects on knowledge institutions (Chapter 6).

It is hard to be cheerful about much of this, but my purpose is to show that – to adapt a famous phrase – another university is possible. The final chapters examine paths of change. There is a much richer history of alternative, experimental and reform universities than we usually realize. This is practical experience, and is a tremendous and fascinating resource (Chapter 7). Yet it needs to be re-thought in the world of the internet, million-dollar vice-chancellors, and trillion-dollar student debt. In Chapter 8 I bring the argument together to define a good university – and equally important, a good university system. We are not cursed forever with the current models; we can design universities worth building, and think practically about how to build them. This does not mean working in an enclave. Universities are linked to the state, the economy, the public culture and the wider education system. Creating good universities implies a broad agenda of democratic change.

I belong to the generation that grew up with The Bomb, aware that we had an excellent chance of exterminating humanity by high-technology war. The current generation knows we are poisoning the planet and may exterminate humanity through climate change. We desperately need ways to generate better futures. Universities are often politically and socially conformist, and neoliberal management is making them more boring by the day. But as bearers of a research-based knowledge formation, and responsible for education at the most advanced levels, university workers must be concerned with challenges to received ideas.

I have worked in universities for fifty years. I am not nostalgic: there never was a golden age when struggle was not needed. I have stuck with universities because their capacity for challenge, critique, invention and intellectual growth survived. I think it is still alive; but it has to be fought for. That is the basic reason for this book.

Chapter 1

Making the knowledge: research

Universities' prestige in the world depends heavily on the work of researchers. Their discoveries are supposed to spark new technologies, deepen our understanding of the world, and guide the work of professions. Graduation addresses proclaim the dignity of science, and the media thrill to the professor with the latest cure for cancer or the most distant galaxy yet found. The World Bank, no less, has proclaimed that we are living in, or at least constructing, Knowledge Societies.

As a matter of fact the knowledge used in everyday practice by clinicians, engineers, and other professions only slightly overlaps with cutting-edge research. Mostly the professions use well-established findings mixed with on-the-job know-how. I have a friend in the medical profession who laments how difficult it is to get doctors to change their prescribing habits when new research comes through. Armand Mattelart and Mats Alvesson have looked coolly into ideas like the 'information society' and the 'knowledge society' and have found a mass of marketing hype and grandiose speculation on top of some real economic changes. Yet even these changes, and the professions' use of well-established findings, show that research-based knowledge matters in the long run.[1]

To understand universities we need to cut through the rhetoric and examine how research-based knowledge is actually made and circulated. Our popular images of intellectuals are isolated geniuses – Dr Faustus with his pentagram, Dr Freud with his cigar, Professor Einstein with his hair. But with few exceptions, modern research involves the interlocking efforts of a whole workforce: not just the star professors but more importantly the research team, graduate students, technical staff, the other research teams, journals, institutes, funding agencies, and more.

Research is a social process, a collective undertaking that produces, not just individual sparks of genius, but an expanding, many-sided, and above all *shared* body of knowledge. I call this product the *research-based knowledge formation*, and later in the chapter I will outline its main features. They give us a way of approaching the difficult but unavoidable question of truth. In an environment of 'post-truth' politics, with trolling, distortion and fakery rampant on the internet, what standing can universities' research-based knowledge have?

Before these questions, we need to understand the work that produces knowledge: the labour process of research. And before that, we need to meet the people who do the work: the researchers themselves, in the global periphery as well as in the famous research centres of the global North.

Being a researcher

I have been a researcher all my working life – mostly part-time, since my jobs have involved teaching too. On some projects I was a lone researcher, including my PhD thesis on how children learn about politics, a sometimes disturbing, sometimes hilarious research topic. But even while writing a one-researcher thesis I was learning about the customs of a larger workforce. At the same time I was involved in team projects, one about class patterns in Australian society and another about teenagers' lives and education. I have been involved in collaborative work ever since, giving some of the most thrilling, as well as the most difficult, moments in my research life.

Collaborative research totally undermines the calm, ivory-tower image of universities. An active research team may have half a dozen projects running at the same time, meanwhile searching for funds for the next half-dozen. Even within one project, as Chief Investigator I find myself doing personnel work with the right hand, data-gathering with the left, scratching my head about theory (with the third hand, of course), then dancing around to fix a hole in the budget. Every grant proposal is an exercise in speculative fiction that closes its eyes to the chaos that is sure to arrive. And only a fraction of the chaos is the creative part. In a survey of 500 Australian intellectual workers in the year 2000, we asked academics, professionals and others to estimate the time they spent on different tasks. On average, 'doing creative work' accounted for less than a quarter of their time.[2]

Budgets are tougher in other regions. The economist Thandika Mkandawire describes researchers in post-independence Africa beset by marginality, under-resourcing and insecurity. Their work depends on erratic funding support from the local state or from international aid agencies. These funders do not want theoretical studies. They want applied research on immediate problems; and what they fund is mostly small-scale, and far from cutting-edge. Mkandawire tartly remarks that donors assumed that 'poor research was good enough for the poor'.[3]

In any region, being a researcher means steering through an institutional environment in a way that allows the logic of knowledge creation to emerge. More than pure intellect is involved: no researcher is just a brain in a glass jar. Researchers have emotions, bodies and relationships.

Consider the fact that researchers have bodies. Some of their labour is fine, healthy work in the open air, such as scrambling up and down hillsides to collect botanical specimens. Some involves travel through lively and varied social environments: for instance ethnographic research in schools. But in any environment, repetitious data-gathering becomes tiring, and ultimately boring. And a lot of research is done in worse surroundings: a laboratory smelling of chemicals, a dust-laden archive, an unsewered field site. Since the 1950s, when computers began to spread through rich countries' universities, more and more of researchers' time has been spent with these machines. At first we wrote on coding sheets, made punch-cards and lugged them across campus to the main-frame computer; now we just sit in front of screens. A long day staring at a screen is seriously unhealthy.

But a lot of researchers spend long days doing just that. They have to. They are subject to deadlines, funding trouble, the irregular rhythms of project-based work, delays and frustrations in the research itself, and the tensions of reviewing and auditing. A considerable part of today's research workforce, probably a majority, are in insecure employment. They are graduate students, grant-funded research assistants, outsourced technical workers, fixed-term research fellows, and untenured academics.[4]

Why put up with these pressures? Earning a living and trying to build a career is an important part of it, and I will discuss the workforce issues in Chapter 3. Beyond this, many researchers believe that their work is intrinsically important. They may not expect to win a Nobel Prize, but they understand that making a contribution to knowledge is a public service, creating an asset for the whole society. Most researchers in universities have a broad commitment to the 'knowledge commons', to use a term from current debates about the internet.

Then there is the fascination of enquiry itself. It is a privilege to spend a working life simply trying to make discoveries. In his charming book *Seed to Seed*, tracing a year in the life of a plant biologist, Nicholas Harberd regrets that you cannot describe this fascination in a journal article: 'Whilst wonder is what really drives us, and wonder is what we feel, we cannot admit of it.'[5] Yet the wonder is real, and sometimes it does break through. Here is a passage from a high-impact research report:

> It is interesting to contemplate a tangled bank, clothed with many plants of many kinds, with birds singing on the bushes, with various insects flitting about, and with worms crawling through the damp earth, and to reflect that these elaborately constructed forms, so different from each other, and dependent upon each other in so complex a manner, have all been produced by laws acting around us … There is grandeur in this view of life, with its several powers, having been originally breathed by the Creator into a few forms or into one; and that, whilst this planet has gone cycling on according to the fixed law of gravity, from so simple a beginning endless forms most beautiful and most wonderful have been, and are being evolved.

I cannot resist quoting that, with its graceful bow to Isaac Newton and its fond picture of the everyday richness of life. It is from the final paragraph of Charles Darwin's *Origin of Species*.[6]

Research has its moments when a bold experiment works, a theory crystallizes, or a solution to the problem is found. Eugene, a senior academic, described such moments in his research in pure mathematics:

> If you've been working on something for a time, you can see things falling into place. And you see this is the right way of doing it. A bit of instinct goes into these things, but you get to know the situation pretty well. And if you have a sudden glimpse of illumination as to how things go, then you're pretty sure it's going to work. Sometimes that doesn't work out of course. But quite often it does.[7]

The glimpse of illumination may turn into the buzz of a hot field. For most knowledge workers the everyday experience is not at that pitch of intensity. But it can involve deep satisfaction, stepping into a researchable zone and finding a path forward in it.

Continuing commitment from a whole workforce makes the research-based knowledge formation possible. This workforce *is* the collective intellectual: a real group of people, spread across the world, whose work depends on sustained cooperation. The emotional dimension is crucial in enabling that. Many researchers work long hours, despite insecurity and frustration. Research groups and networks provide friendship, mentoring, collaboration, advice, and help in crises.

In a pioneering analysis of intellectual workers, Geoff Sharp observed that their work required autonomy, and tended to organize itself as a horizontal network of people linked by cooperation rather than command. These ideas have become common, and do have some empirical support. In our survey of 500 Australian intellectual workers, we asked for responses to the statement *Most people in my workplace treat each other as equals.* No less than 81 per cent agreed and only 14 per cent disagreed.[8]

But there was systematic variation. It is very thought-provoking that the university workers in this survey, compared with other sectors, scored *low* on a scale measuring autonomy in the workplace. At the bottom of the research economy, the work is more likely to be routine, the autonomy minimal and the pay poor. The famous experiments on air pressure and chemicals in the seventeenth century, which we attribute to the Honourable Robert Boyle and his friends, were actually carried out by the philosophical gentlemen's servants, not named as authors. Bonnie, a contemporary Australian industrial chemist, worked for a while as a laboratory research assistant at her university. She bitterly remarked of her experience:

Look, a well-trained monkey can do this work.

Bonnie left her field and left the university, despite getting her PhD and winning a post-doctoral fellowship. I have spoken with researchers in the global South who felt with similar anger that, in certain international projects, they had been little more than recruitment agents for global-North researchers.[9]

There are, indeed, steep global hierarchies. Europe and North America hold most of the celebrity researchers, leading journals and research funds. I will discuss global inequalities in a later chapter, but want to register from the start that the research-based knowledge formation floats on a highly unequal and politically unstable world economy. It has no guarantee of security.

The work of research

In 1892 Karl Pearson, a founder of modern statistics (who later vanished into the crank science of eugenics), published a widely-read book called *The Grammar of Science*. This laid out an empiricist vision:

> We have defined the scientific method to consist in the orderly classification of facts followed by the recognition of their relationship and recurring sequences. The scientific judgment is the judgment based upon this recognition and free from personal bias.[10]

The key word here is 'orderly', and Pearson's book is just one of a whole genre that tries to define science's traffic rules. Some like Pearson emphasize the facts or data, others like the Vienna Circle philosophers of the 1920s emphasize hypotheses, laws and their verification or falsification. But all think there is a definite rationality governing the work of researchers. It is expressed in the very title of Karl Popper's 1934 classic

Logik der Forschung, the Logic of Research. To these stern thinkers, the logic sharply separates true science from religion, magic, metaphysics, opinion ('personal bias'), and other fluff.[11]

But there is an opposing view, stated with great verve a generation later by the philosopher Paul Feyerabend. To him, any rationalist model of science is a dangerous illusion. The reality is epistemological anarchism: 'The only principle that does not inhibit progress is: *anything goes*.' The famous quantum physicist Richard Feynman makes a similar argument against pre-determined rules:

> What is necessary 'for the very existence of science', and what the characteristics of nature are, are not to be determined by pompous preconditions, they are determined always by the material with which we work, by nature herself. We look, and we see what we can find, and we cannot say ahead of time successfully what it is going to look like.[12]

The crucial point is the capacity of the knowledge formation to grow. Taking Galileo as his example, Feyerabend argues that actual scientific advances do not follow traffic rules. In this he is surely right. Advancing knowledge is a messy, unpredictable process. In a recent history of the European scientific revolution of the sixteenth and seventeenth centuries, David Wootton emphasizes that the very idea of 'discovery' of things unknown was a key element in the new cultural pattern.[13]

What is missing from most of the epistemological debate is the social and economic organization of research. However things were done in the time of Galileo, the making of knowledge is now a global industry with a large labour force. A large industry does not work only by anarchic impulses. Research combines different forms of work and different groups of workers. This is a composite labour process, with elements of chaos and unpredictability, but not randomly assembled.

There is a social logic that emerges when we think about the whole collective enterprise of constructing new knowledge.

The process starts, ironically, by looking at old knowledge. PhD students are usually told to write a 'literature review' at the start of their thesis, where they summarize earlier research. Many wonder why. It may seem a pointless ritual; in fact it is vital. What research does is transform an existing state of knowledge into a new state. The more deeply the existing knowledge is understood, the better. I call this *archive* work.

This used to be called scholarship. One thinks of the grey-haired professor coughing over books deep in the library stacks. It's not a myth – I've done some of that coughing myself – though scholarship now means searches on the desktop computer more often than on dusty shelves. As well as the literature, the archive also includes the skills that have crystallized in earlier research. There is accumulated knowledge of how to make a bubble chamber work, how to excavate a prehistoric site, how to do a field interview and so forth.

The archive is vital, but research does not reproduce it. Rather, research moves *from* the archive. A mist-covered, researchable zone spreads out just ahead of what we currently know in any field. Defining a researchable question is a hidden art in research, very difficult to teach. Essentially, it's a matter of finding a path forward through the mist, into that zone. Every research plan therefore faces two ways, pointing back to the archive from which it starts, and pointing forward to the new knowledge it hopes to make. Don't be surprised that this planning is often laborious and slow!

Discovering things is what most people mean by 'research', and this is the work that grants committees mostly fund: tramping the hills and collecting the seeds, finding the clay tablets in the ruins, taking the blood samples from the patients, poring over the manuscripts. It can be done on a screen, such as the biomedical research that trawls big datasets already assembled. It can be romantic, even today: think of Antarctic research, where you have to travel by ship or plane to a remote and dangerous environment. Wherever it is done, I call this part of the process *encounter.*

This happens in the humanities as consistently as in the natural and social sciences. Some commentators claim there is no 'research' in the humanities, which are all about interpretation. But since interpretation must have materials to interpret, the work of encounter is done there too. Only a painfully narrow definition of research would exclude a scholarly edition of Shakespeare, a study of artistic styles or a wrestle with philosophies of justice.[14]

The repetitive parts of encounter-work are often handed to the junior members of a research team. In some fields, like atmospheric science, data collection is now largely automated. Andrew Pickering's book *The Mangle of Practice* is one of the best accounts of what actually happens in research. He emphasizes the machine culture in physical science, and describes how strange machines like the bubble chamber were developed. But he also emphasizes the human work that is needed – calibrating, modifying, adjusting, which may take years – before the machines deliver meaningful results.[15]

In the encounter with materials, the world answers in its own way. We may have excellent guesses as to what is out there, but as Feynman rightly says, we do not know in advance. The fossils are what they are, and when questioned in a new way, they may give answers that overthrow current knowledge. Exactly that happened in a celebrated report in palaeontology, H. B. Whittington's monograph 'The enigmatic animal *Opabinia regalis*'. Intensive microscopic scrutiny of these 500-million-year-old invertebrate fossils, fifty years after they were found in the Burgess shale in Canada, revealed a creature that had been badly misinterpreted, and brought existing classifications into question.[16]

To learn from the materials we must respect them. Careful recording of the encounters is vital, whether in the battered black notebook or the brave new data matrix in the Cloud. There is good reason to be careful. In every encounter with materials, researchers are putting their own ideas, and the accumulated knowledge in their field, at risk.

As the materials accumulate, the researchers try to understand them, i.e. to produce intellectual structures that show patterns in the materials. We speak of interpretations, theories or models. I call this work *patterning*. It always goes beyond the given. As Einstein put it, 'the compilation of a classified catalogue' is not the whole of science: intuition and deductive thought are also needed.[17]

Patterning involves imagination; boldness is a virtue here. Yet the boldness is sharply constrained by the resistance of the world. Patterning requires familiarity with the materials, a sense of their texture and shape. The German language has a lovely word for this: *Fingerspitzengefühl*, finger-tip feeling, combining sensitivity and flair. All good researchers have it, though it is hard to convey in the stilted language of journals.

Patterning has varied genres. Newton's and Boyle's generation made mathematics the most prestigious way of expressing patterns in the physical world. A climate model today may be an immense string of differential equations written in a million lines of computer code. In a clinical field, the pattern may be expressed as a statement of where a patient sits in a classification, such as the American Psychiatric Association's famous *Diagnostic and Statistical Manual*. In literary studies, history, ethnography or philosophy, the pattern may be expressed in a book of dense prose. A classic example is Jacqueline de Romilly's monograph *Histoire et raison chez Thucydide* (translated as *The Mind of Thucydides*), which revealed the logic hidden within a famous ancient text, and re-shaped a whole field of research.[18]

Patterning describes the material in a form distinct from the original record of the encounters. In fields such as physics this statement is much more economical, but not in all fields. The key point is that patterning links cases, connects up different encounters. That is what makes research intellectually powerful.

The statement of a pattern also defines limits to what is known. At the end of all my research projects, I have been left with heaps of information beyond what I could interpret and take to a journal. Research not only increases our knowledge, it also constantly reveals our ignorance. The abundance and splendour of science should never lead to arrogance.[19]

At the end of the ideal journal article, after the Literature Review, Hypotheses, Method and Findings, comes the Conclusion. Authors often skimp this, hurrying on to the next paper or the next grant application. But they should not. This is where they formulate the step they have just taken beyond the archive, beyond current knowledge. However small the contribution of a particular project, it is *this* piece of work that gives the knowledge formation as a whole its distinctive capacity to grow. This is the moment when a new reality, a new state of knowledge, comes into being.

I call this piece of work *critique*, since revising the archive is the essence of growth. Nothing is exempt from critique, not even the data. In biology, for instance, a lot of work goes into mapping the distribution of plant and animal species: very important for understanding ecosystems. But down the corridor, the taxonomists are also at work. Their studies may show that what was formerly understood as one species is actually two or more; or that creatures formerly labelled separate species actually belong to the same one. In either case, the earlier data on distribution become questionable, even unusable.[20]

In critique, boldness is not a virtue: honest appraisal is. The work of critique expresses a collective modesty. All findings, all theories, are provisional. I have found it sobering to go back into the dust and read the dreadful stuff researchers in my field were writing a hundred years ago. I blench to think what any reader a hundred years hence will think of my stuff ...

The most brilliant fieldwork, theory or critique would go for nothing if the world does not hear about them. Research is a highly social process, even when a researcher is working solo. The findings have to be taken to the people who can use them. I call this work *broadcasting* rather than 'publication', to emphasize its open-ended character. It is integral to the research process itself, because this work creates the archive of knowledge.

Broadcasting to other researchers takes the form of conference papers, books, stand-alone reports and journal articles. There are about 35 000 research journals in the world, and more appear all the time. Research journals began as the printed minutes of early scientific societies, plus the letters they received from other researchers. They have become standardized now, but more imaginative forms exist. An influential twentieth-century study of central African language was written by Alexis Kagamé in the form of a Platonic dialogue. Three centuries ago Galileo used the dialogue form for astronomy.

Equally important is broadcasting to professions and wider publics. Biomedical research is put into digests for clinicians. Mass media have a role, sometimes surprising. Michael Ventris first published the decipherment of Linear B, the mysterious writing on clay tablets from prehistoric Greece, as a radio talk on the BBC. The internet is busily producing new genres now, such as blog posts and online databanks.[21]

Whatever the genre, writing well is skilled labour. There is a mass of bad writing in research journals, because of condensation and haste. A lot of academics are more focussed on pumping out papers than on thinking how they communicate. 'Performance management' in universities makes this worse. The problem can be solved, but only by returning to the basic social logic of research-based knowledge.

To summarize all this, research directly involves five main types of labour: using the archive, encountering materials, patterning, critique and broadcasting. I could present them as a cycle, since broadcasting creates the archive. But that would be misleading. All these steps depend on another layer of work, done by the operations staff. Administrative, professional and maintenance workers keep the institutions running and keep the research staff paid, supplied and safe.

Further, as every experienced researcher knows, the five types of labour are interwoven in daily practice. There is not a neat sequence or cycle. Patterning and critique often begin together at the stage of research design. Writing is done from beginning to end of a research project. Critique is on researchers' minds all the time. A journal article presents a research project neatly, but schematically. In crude reality, conducting the project is always messier, more complicated, and more creative.

The knowledge formation

Research-based knowledge comes out of a complex labour process. The workforce is diverse, the methods are varied, the organization is anarchic, the results are unpredictable. Why doesn't it all fly apart?

The answer is in the social process. From many beginnings, through a complex institutional history, and across a global geography, research-based knowledge has become connected and formalized. In the last two centuries it has gelled into a full-scale knowledge formation. By a knowledge formation I mean a socially organized body of information, concepts, methods, norms of truth, genres of communication, and applications; persisting through time, and capable of developing itself. A knowledge formation, in other words, is an episteme in its practical existence.

There are multiple knowledge formations in the world today, and there have been others in the past. Newman's *Idea of a University* was a bad plan for a new university because it looked backward to a dying knowledge formation, one that depended on orthodox religion and centred on the study of ancient texts. Newman's close contemporary, the unorthodox French philosopher Auguste Comte, looked forward and became the most influential theorist of the research-based knowledge formation. Comte's map of knowledge, devised in the 1830s when he was a fairly young man, still influences university curriculum and organization today.

In his *Cours de philosophie positive* Comte laid out a hierarchy of sciences based on their objects of knowledge and on the dependence of one science on another. In his scheme, the 'positive' sciences were five. Astronomy, physics, and chemistry all dealt with the inorganic world at different levels of complexity. In the organic world there were two levels: physiology (what we call biological science) and social physics or sociology (what we call social science). It was crucial that Comte placed the sciences of life and society in the same sequence as the sciences of inorganic nature. Before this sequence came mathematics, on which all the rest depended. The result was six grand domains of knowledge, making a coherent, beautifully ordered curriculum.[22]

Comte was a truly terrible writer; reading his prose is like wading through wet cement. But this conception was very powerful. By the end of the nineteenth century the idea of an ordered realm of research-based knowledge could be taken for granted, and this was the framework that universities needed. The research-based knowledge formation and the research university now developed together.

James Frazer's classic of armchair anthropology *The Golden Bough*, first published in 1890, contrasted magic, religion and science as knowledge formations and plumped for science:

> The abundance, the solidity, and the splendour of the results already achieved by science are well fitted to inspire us with a cheerful confidence in the soundness of its method. Here at last, after groping about in the dark for countless ages, man has hit upon a clue to the labyrinth, a golden key that opens many locks in the treasury of nature.[23]

More than a century later this abundance is still celebrated in triumphalist rhetoric about technology, innovation, and science-driven growth and prosperity. Frazer in his armchair was a little more wary. He thought a time would come when this golden key would be replaced by some other, still unimagined, form of knowledge.

The research-based knowledge formation has two distinctive features. First, it is public – relentlessly public, in principle. Lectures and conferences are public events (especially with the audience on Twitter). Concepts and findings are always open to debate, and 'publication' is considered a vital step in research. There are no facts or doctrines known only to initiates. It may be difficult to get up to speed: you may have to learn another language, some complex mathematics, or a subtle analytic technique. But in principle anyone can do it, and the more who do it, the better. In the logic of research-based knowledge, there is a democratic core.

The public character of knowledge is often under pressure. Corporate interests are now entrenched in research publishing, and there is a struggle for open access. Religious and political authorities have often used their power to protect orthodox beliefs and the regime in power. Social science in China, for instance, is scrutinized by the regime, and little that is subversive gets through. The United States in the 1940s tried to keep secret its research for the atomic bomb, as all regimes that own atomic weapons still try to do. Of course secrets leak, partly by espionage – but partly by reading the publications. At the height of the Second World War the physicist Georgy Flyorov, then in the Soviet air force, visited a university library and noticed that nuclear research had vanished from the US journals. He deduced what was going on, alerted his senior colleagues, got no support there, and finally in frustration wrote direct to Stalin. His campaign helped shift professional and political opinion, and from 1943 the scientific talent of the Soviet Union too was working, in secrecy, towards nuclear weapons.[24]

The second distinctive feature is that research-based knowledge is constantly changing. Other knowledge formations change and adapt, but this one has a distinctive pace of change. It exists in its endless re-creation, and draws its authority, not from elders, traditions or foundational texts, but precisely from its capacity for invention and re-making.

That is what the Nobel Prizes are awarded for. Alfred Nobel's will, written just five years after the first edition of *The Golden Bough*, declared:

> The said interest shall be divided into five equal parts, which shall be apportioned as follows: one part to the person who shall have made the most important discovery or invention within the field of physics; one part to the person who shall have made the most important chemical discovery or improvement; one part to the person who shall have made the most important discovery within the domain of physiology or medicine ...[25]

It is not by chance that media reporting of research constantly trumpets 'breakthroughs', nor that modern epistemology has been so fascinated by scientific revolutions.

Knowledge workers themselves have an acute awareness of change. In the Australian survey of knowledge workers mentioned earlier, we asked their reaction to the statement *In my field of work, knowledge and methods are changing rapidly*. Some 83 per cent agreed and only 15 per cent disagreed. Agreement was higher in historically new fields; but even in old-established fields of knowledge, three-quarters of the respondents agreed with this statement. What Thomas Kuhn in his famous book *The Structure of Scientific Revolutions* rather disparagingly called 'normal science', i.e. research within a paradigm, is far from static. The norm is a collective process of change.[26]

But if the knowledge formation is constantly in a state of change, what reliance can be placed in it? Are the climate change deniers right, that scientists are making fools of the public? Where is the solidity and splendour that Frazer invoked?

The answer has to do with the collective character of intellectual work. It is not just one researcher, one project or one finding that represents the state of knowledge. Rather it is a growing mass of findings produced by a whole workforce of researchers, and especially the way the findings are linked up, as fields of knowledge unfold and influence each other. The collective labour of research brings a social reality – the knowledge formation as a whole – into existence, through historical time.[27]

Mostly this process is taken for granted, but sometimes it becomes visible. Consider this extract from an interview with Tim, a high-profile medical researcher who had returned to Australia after a period in the United States:

> I knew just about everybody who was a leading [worker in this field] in America before I left, and with many have become good friends. And we set up this project, this think-tank which I'm going off to in a couple of weeks, we're having our seventh meeting. And what I enjoy most about that is that we get some of the top people in the field together. Mainly Americans, but we have a couple, one from Sweden, one from England, one from Denmark, but it's mainly Americans. And what we do is, we map out a series of questions that need to be answered. And then we say 'Jack you do this', 'John you do this'. We'll meet again next March and report back.[28]

In his own field, Tim is a member of the network at the leading edge of research. He and his colleagues are strategizing for the growth of that whole field and its workforce.

The research-based knowledge formation changes in structure. Even in Comte's day, no-one could master the curriculum as a whole. As the nineteenth and twentieth centuries advanced, the overcrowding became desperate, and more and more specialized disciplines were defined and separated from one another. In 1936 the young and enthusiastic President of the University of Chicago, Robert Maynard Hutchins, published *The Higher Learning in America* complaining bitterly of the resulting anarchy of academic life. He proposed a dramatic purge and re-unification of the university based on – of all things – Aristotle's metaphysics. Even Newman might have flinched. To nobody's surprise, Hutchins could not persuade his professors to adopt this scheme.[29]

More recent studies of academic life portray different disciplinary cultures in fields like literature, mathematics, engineering and sociology – perhaps even exaggerating the differences. Associations and conferences that cover the whole spectrum of knowledge have been dying. The long-standing Australian and New Zealand Association for the Advancement of Science, for instance, collapsed about twenty-five years ago.

In turn, the disciplines have briskly sub-divided themselves. The American Sociological Association currently has 52 specialized sections, from 'Aging and the Life Course' via 'Ethnomethodology and Conversation Analysis' and 'Global and Transnational Sociology' all the way to 'Theory'. And the sociologists are not the worst offenders. The meta-journal *Mathematical Reviews*, intended to survey current research output in mathematics, needs a closely-printed 47-page document, endearingly called *MSC2010*, just to list the hundreds of topics that the *Reviews* cover. Each one can be a specialty – from 'Philosophy of Mathematics' through traditional areas like 'Number Theory' to the potentially explosive new field of 'Econophysics', involving applications of quantum mechanics to economics.[30]

Funding agencies such as the European Union have tried to counter this fragmentation by rewarding interdisciplinary projects. Some fusions have appeared more organically. Physical chemistry is an old one, molecular biology a newer one, climate change science newer again.

Some startling connections between disciplines do get made. I once read an admirable paper on the botany of the motor vehicle. Some clever botanists had gone to a car-wash and collected the seeds, pollen and plant fragments that automobiles were carrying around – a new wrinkle on the biogeography of invasive species. There is now a research literature based on car-wash data! On a larger scale, whole swathes of historical research have been reconfigured by nuclear physics. Carbon-14 dating is based on the fact that different isotopes of carbon exist in the wood, ash and other organic material left in archaeological sites. Calculations based on the rate of decay of the radioactive isotope Carbon-14 give probable dates for sites far older than the earliest written records. Other physics-based methods, such as thermoluminescence dating, have now expanded the field.[31]

The mistake that Hutchins made, and perhaps the European Union too, was to look for unity in the state of knowledge at a given point of time. A fragile order can be imposed by funding agencies and university managements, but that will be only temporary. What holds the knowledge formation together is the collective, historically unfolding process itself, the social logic of the labour that we call research. The element of anarchy and instability is not a weakness. It is inherent in a creative, democratic process of making, testing and circulating knowledge.

Research and truth

> What is truth? said jesting Pilate; and would not stay for an answer.

Thus Francis Bacon opened his essay 'Of truth', citing a biblical story all his readers would know. As well as being an important political figure in Renaissance England, Bacon was one of the first philosophers to discuss the research-based knowledge formation. In 1620 he published an empiricist manifesto, *Novum Organum Scientiarum* (the title gestures towards replacing Aristotle's treatises on method, the *Organon*). Its most memorable section is Bacon's cr[illegible] of the various 'idols' – of the tribe, of the cave, of the market and of the theatre – that lead judgment astray and obscure the truth.

To speak of truth at all is to enter dangerous ground. Quite apart from the bitterness of 'post-truth politics', this is one of the most worked-over terms in philosophy. There are knotty problems about evidence, objectivity and probability statements. Lorraine Daston and Peter Galison have shown that the meaning of objectivity in science changed quite dramatically over time. There are long-running debates about how to define truth; indeed, whether it can be defined at all outside highly formalized logics. The United Nations General Assembly has asserted a 'Right to the Truth', but only about human rights violations. Perhaps Pontius Pilate, no enthusiast for human rights, was wise not to wait.[32]

Yet the idea of truth remains powerful and necessary, and perhaps not too mysterious. I am encouraged by Steven Shapin's fascinating book *A Social History of Truth*, which shows how truth-telling and verification in early experimental physics grew out of the social code of trust and courtesy among the English gentry of the time. I am also encouraged by Liam Hudson's book *The Cult of the Fact*, a charming but ruthless dissection of empiricism which includes – as far as I know – the only defence of unicorns in modern psychology. Hudson's main point is to show how intellectual orthodoxies in university departments stifle the imagination that good research needs.[33]

If there were a simple, direct correspondence between observations of the world and the declarations that circulate as research findings, there would hardly be a problem. But there is no such correspondence. Theories and measurements have to condense, abstracting from the details of observation. There is often an excess of data – but sometimes too little. Observation itself is normally theory-laden. In a number of disciplines today, including climate science, cosmology, population genetics and macro-economics, research is largely carried out through mathematical modelling. This process does not attempt point-by-point correspondence with observations. Rather, it takes a set of observations and assumptions as starting-points and then generates, via calculations that often require huge computing power, a set of probability statements as outcomes. These will be compared with new data, in a restless process of refining and elaborating the models.

A defining principle of the whole knowledge formation is that knowledge should transform and grow. This principle rules out any idea of truth as fixed. In the research-based formation, truth can only operate as a criterion for the practices through which knowledge is transformed.

Though it is a common expression, we cannot say that in research we are trying to find the truth, as if we were looking for the South Pole, or a good restaurant. We can say, and it is more precise to say, that we are trying to work *in a truthful way*. We are trying to create knowledge that can be trusted, used and reliably built on, in a continuing social process. Truth in research, then, is closely bound up with the making of a knowledge commons. In a university context, this means the body of knowledge (and the methods for making it) held in trust by a research community as a whole.[34]

Working truthfully is a strong requirement. Over time, researchers have evolved practical ways of arriving at trustworthy findings. Some are quite simple, others more complicated. They include:

- Keeping accurate records of the encounter with materials. For instance, recording each step in an archaeological excavation, not just the showy jewellery but also the humble fragments of clay pots, and their exact places in the soil.
- Being concerned with the fullness of information. For instance, getting complete sets or representative samples

of populations (in surveys), of documents (in historical studies) or of research literature (in meta-analyses).

- Testing findings by running the research again, especially by another researcher. This is not a prestigious activity, and it is not easy to replicate a study exactly. There is now sharp debate in psychology about how replicable most research is.[35]
- Paying attention to the applications of research. Do the patients recover? Do the children learn? Do the crops grow? These may not be decisive tests, since there are many reasons for these outcomes, but they are relevant.
- Checking the quality of research before it is published. The most famous practice here is peer review, which is often presented as a truth-guarantee.

Essentially, peer reviewing is a way to make organizational decisions affecting research: whether to grant research funds; whether to use a journal's resources to publish a paper. It has its downside: it may protect orthodoxy and privilege, like a club defending its turf. The sociologist Michèle Lamont has recently shown, in a fly-on-the-wall study of national grants committees in the United States, that even in this very privileged environment peer review is a highly pragmatic business. It involves much negotiation, though the scholars Lamont studied try to follow norms of breadth and open-mindedness.[36]

Peer review only gradually emerged as a custom. Perhaps the most famous journal article of all, Albert Einstein's 1905 paper 'On the electrodynamics of moving bodies' – the first statement of relativity theory – was never peer reviewed. It was published on the judgment of the associate editor of *Annalen der Physik* at the time, Max Planck, who knew the young man's work. Peer review is not the gold standard of truth. It is simply one of the devices to encourage trustworthy knowledge.

The rhetoric of research is easy to counterfeit. Isaac Asimov, when he was a PhD student in chemistry, wrote an excellent article, 'The endochronic properties of resublimated thiotimoline', which reported experiments on a little-known chemical that was so extremely soluble that it dissolved just *before* it was put into water.

Asimov's article was a joke. No such thing as 'thiotimoline' exists. The article was actually published in the magazine *Astounding Science Fiction*, and the chemistry student went on to a fine career as a novelist. But there was no joking in the fabricated data recently circulated in peer-reviewed papers by the social psychologist Diederik Stapel. Nor in the twin-study data put out a couple of generations earlier by the politically conservative psychologist Cyril Burt, which for a long time passed as proof that IQ was hereditary, thus supporting class and race biases in education.[37]

Nor is there much amusing in the drug-company-funded biomedical research that so persistently reports good effects for the drugs those companies wish to market. Nor in the barrage of misrepresentation and the forged documents in David Irving's widely circulated books about Nazi Germany and the Second World War, which are demolished step by step in the historian Richard Evans' disturbing volume *Telling Lies about Hitler*. Nor in the 'virtual social science', as the sociologist Judith Stacey calls it, in which opponents of gay marriage cherry-pick a little data that suits them while ignoring the main findings of the research on parenting. Nor in the Japanese/Chinese standoff about whether the 1937–38 massacres known as the Rape of Nanking actually happened; nor in the fundamentalist attacks on evolutionary biology, which continue to this day; nor in the media and government attacks on historians who documented the frontier killings of Aborigines in Australia.[38]

We need to pay attention to such cases so we do not get complacent about the solidity and splendour of science. Research-based knowledge is under pressure from many sides. To resist that pressure, it is very helpful to have a vigorous concept of truth. All the cases of denialism and distortion just listed have been challenged. Richard Evans considers the controversy about Irving and Nazism, which came to a head in a libel trial, as a test of whether historians can establish truth. He concludes that they can, through the kind of practices I have listed above: comprehensiveness in the search for evidence, corrigibility and self-criticism in argument, and accuracy in documentation and reporting.[39]

That is encouraging. But there is another problem, which lies deeper. Truthfulness in research is an aspect of the social process of making knowledge and is connected with the making of a knowledge commons. The whole knowledge formation, as I argued earlier in the chapter, comes from the labour of a research workforce. But what if that workforce is highly unrepresentative; what if knowledge institutions work in an exclusionary way; what if the knowledge economy embeds privilege and exploitation on a global scale? Readers may have noticed that the famous figures mentioned in this chapter so far are, overwhelmingly, white bourgeois men from western Europe and North America.

Several traditions of critical thought have argued that the social conditions of intellectual work do affect knowledge. Gyorgy Lukács' powerful *History and Class Consciousness*, published in 1923 (and immediately suppressed by authoritarians both right and left), put the socialist case that the class privilege of philosophers set fundamental limits to what bourgeois philosophy could know. Feminist critics from the Women's Liberation movement showed that men's domination of the university world is reflected in both curriculum and research; whole realms of women's experience have been excluded from the kingdom of organized knowledge. Indigenous and postcolonial critics have documented the privilege of elite institutions in the global North, the unequal world trade in information, and the exclusion or marginalization of knowledge formations from the global South.[40]

These issues will concern us throughout the book. They have no quick solutions, since they involve major social structures. Yet I will say immediately that the key resource against the lies and distortions discussed earlier, the public character of research-based knowledge, is also relevant here. Good research practice not only involves fidelity to materials and completeness of information, it also involves social responsibility. Hence the importance of a public realm where that responsibility can be exercised. Hence the importance of a democratic culture in the knowledge formation. Working in a truthful way requires that distorted thinking, privileges, exclusions and outright lies should be contested. Truth is a critical concept. That is essential to keep in mind, because significant pressures against truth now come from universities themselves.

Chapter 2

Learning and teaching

Most people who have been students at a university will remember arriving for their first classes: the uncertainty of a new start, the thrill of a new freedom, the hope of discovering new things. This is *higher* education at last. Students will work at advanced levels of knowledge, and in research universities they will be taught by people who actually make the knowledge. In professional degrees they will learn how knowledge is put to use in the wider world. In social life they will meet more people than they did in high school, and more diverse, at least in public universities. They are adults now and can vote, form relationships, stage plays, pray, call demonstrations, or just sit under a tree and think. If they stick it out for several years they will graduate in an impressive ceremony, attended by their teachers in splendid costumes, and will be told their learning is important for the future of the world. Many of their teachers, too, have high hopes – for higher education as moral, cultural and political growth, the idea contained in the untranslatable German word *Bildung*.

How well are those hopes realized? In June 1918 the students of the University of Córdoba in Argentina gave a famous answer to this question. The *Córdoba Declaration*, issued during a wave of demonstrations and a student occupation, denounced the mediocrity and dullness of academic teaching, the conservatism and arrogance of the university authorities, and the lack of a 'spiritual' (we would say 'inspiring') connection between teacher and student. It was a remarkable document, and helped trigger a wave of university reform across Latin America.[1]

In 1970 a young Australian scholar called Graham Little published *The University Experience*, based on detailed interviews with senior students at a large Australian university. It is still one of the best studies of its kind, and it makes sobering reading. Even then, at the height of a radical student movement, in a period often thought the golden age of universities, the majority experience for students was a pragmatic routine of lectures and exams, with remote academics, limited commitment among students, and not much intellectual excitement.[2]

In 2015 a Canadian humanities professor called Ron Srigley published an essay about life in the neoliberal university in North America. It was a picture of even deeper alienation: students texting on their mobile phones in class, academics without interest in teaching, degrees with little solid content. Everyone was going through the motions, while a facade was kept up by grade inflation and deceptive advertising. In the same year Richard Hil published an interview-based study of Australian student life in the era of the market. He called it *Selling Students Short*, and his picture of a drab, routinized and impoverished learning experience is not very different from Graham Little's. As one of his interviewees put it,

> There's no emotional attachment to the place. It's sad but I think most graduating students think this way.[3]

For some students, one must say, the experience is even worse, running into impatient or hostile academics, unfeeling managers and ever-increasing debt. Resentment and anger are also part of the picture.

One reason for these uninspiring scenes is the economic and social design of universities, which I will consider later. But another is the pattern of mainstream teaching, and that will be the main concern of this chapter.

The work of learning

The place to start is where the Córdoba reform started, with the students. In higher education generally, and specifically in universities, the main learning task is engaging with advanced forms of knowledge. What counts as advanced knowledge is largely defined by the research-based knowledge formation, described in the previous chapter.

University students are adults, with adult bodies, endurance and skills; a lot can be asked of them, and they can give a lot. They have adult intellectual capacities, with a great deal of prior learning. Formal learning at university is not about writing new knowledge on a blank page. It is about transforming intellectual structures and skills that the students have already developed. This is work, and the student is the main worker. Paradoxically, the student is also the object of the work. It is the student's own capacities for practice that are being transformed, in any educational process.

This transformation is an active process on the part of the students. In professional degrees, this is clearly acknowledged in the 'practicum'. Students in dentistry, medicine, architecture or education often see this part of the curriculum as getting to the real stuff at last. Under some guidance, they are now actually fronting a classroom and amusing the kids, actually using the drills and scaring the patients. When they get into the profession after graduating, they are likely to find they still have a lot to learn about practice. But the process begins in initial training at university.

Students' engagement and activity are also central to learning in arts and science courses, in the 'theory' part of vocational degrees, and in research higher degrees. You don't learn theory by leaning back and letting a lecture on Hegel wash over you; you learn it by trying to theorize. Engage with Hegel if you must, but remember that the Cunning of Reason advances one step at a time. It is one of the few universal laws I know. To learn, a student has to conduct the intellectual operations for herself, and thus create a structure of knowledge in her own consciousness and practice.

For this reason, as a teacher, I have always tried to bring first-year students into contact with some of the cutting-edge research in their field; and I have tried to give undergraduates, as early as possible, experience of their own research projects. I know they will not yet grasp the fine details. But showing researchers at work, in the sweaty mess of building knowledge, and trying out the research process itself, are the best ways to help students with their own tasks of building knowledge. For that is what the work of learning ultimately involves. Learning is a specific form of the creation of knowledge.

What the students create in the course of their learning will always differ in some details from the conventional views in a discipline, and will include mistakes. There is something very unpleasant about the websites, Facebook pages and newspaper articles that collect students' mistakes and jeer at them. The Murdoch-owned *Times Higher Education* in Britain runs an annual competition, inviting academics to submit the worst howlers. What is troubling here is not only the blatant disrespect for students engaged in a learning process. This attitude trashes an educational resource. Students' mis-understandings provide teachers with important clues to what is happening in the classroom. Even more important, they provide the students with information that helps them steer their own learning, as they learn from their mistakes. Indeed, they need to learn how to *make* mistakes – how to push forward without embarrassment or fear, incorporating false steps and reversals into a complex learning process.

Like research, learning at this level is usually uncertain and slow. We do not get 'one-trial learning' at university. Advanced intellectual work constantly involves re-examining, criticizing and modifying existing structures of knowledge. The process cannot be condensed without being damaged. Current attempts by policymakers and marketers to speed up degrees, to cram a BA into two years and a PhD into three, will – with absolute certainty – make the learning shallower.

One reason it takes time is that being a student involves complex sequences of emotion. Interest, boredom, puzzlement, shock, discouragement, excitement – all in turn are woven through the intellectual processes of learning. Stefan Collini, the British humanist who is one of the most thoughtful commentators on universities, sharply criticizes 'student satisfaction' surveys as measures of teaching quality. He points out that real learning in university *should* be disturbing, because it challenges existing ideas – and that will often be unpleasant. I think he is right. But higher learning should also give joy, and plenty of it. There should be joy in encounter, in creation, in overcoming difficulties, in acquiring insight, even artistic pleasure in the intellectual structures we are learning about.[4]

My best experience as an undergraduate was in a second-year psychological statistics class, of all things. We had been taught in first year to use formulas from the book to calculate correlation coefficients and significance tests. Now we had a teacher with a different approach, who showed us the mathematical logic underlying those formulas. As I began to grasp what he was doing, what had been a mechanical slog opened out as a field of beauty. And, indeed, a field of politics, since the logical construction of the formulas was not itself mechanical, but involved decisions that shaped our representations of the world. I am not a statistician and I did not take the course beyond third year, but I have never been scared of numbers since. Statistics is a beautifully constructed tool, which can do great things when used mindfully!

Students grappling with complex learning tasks need times of solitude – which are necessary for creative work, as the South African novelist Nadine Gordimer has observed. But much of the time there are other students under the tree, at the coffee shop or in the online chat-room. This is important too. Students teach each other. In a well-designed course they circulate learning materials and do research together, as well as joke, advise and encourage each other. They are the most important resource in dealing with stress and emotional crises, which are not rare in student life.[5]

These are powerful processes. When graduates look back on their university experience, it is often the informal student groups that seem most central. An intelligent university would see this as a tremendous asset for higher education, and would do all in its power to support it. I am dismayed, therefore, when I see course guides starting with a mandated page of terrible threats against 'plagiarism'. Indeed copying off the internet without attribution is a waste of everyone's time – but it is a sign of alienation, overwork or language problems, i.e. of a failed educational process. What course guides would be doing, if a university is working well, is encouraging mutual aid and collective learning.

In many ways we can regard the collective, rather than the individual, as the learner. This conflicts with the logic of competitive testing, which focusses on the individual and pits students against each other. But we should acknowledge collective learning processes of some importance, which feature in some of the most inventive university reforms. Collective learning can be linked with a credentialling process, too. When we recognize it, we do more than expand the picture of learning. We view students as part of the active workforce of the knowledge economy – and that matters for a democratic approach to the future of universities.

The course being run

Curriculum, from a Latin word meaning 'running', has come to mean the content of a course of study. (The Latin root also means 'chariot', which suggests an interesting solution to university parking problems.) Curriculum seems a simple matter, laid out for all to see in course guides. Yet it has depths. There is a fascinating historical literature on how subjects like geography, linguistics or medicine were assembled by academic entrepreneurs. Their work made fresh selections and combinations of existing knowledge, accompanied by exclusions and suppressions. The exclusion of women's healing knowledge during the development of modern medical curricula is a famous example.[6]

The official curriculum defines only part of what is learnt. There is also a hidden curriculum taught by organizational structures, daily routines and social interactions. Time spent as a student teaches about dress, friendship, drinking, sexual behaviour, prejudice, and career expectations. In a careful ethnographic study of young women's experiences at two universities in the United States in the 1980s, Dorothy Holland and Margaret Eisenhart found that for most of the students, the academic curriculum had minor importance in daily life. What counted more heavily was the peer-group culture, which steered women's lives towards gendered work and marriage. Holland and Eisenhart ruefully called their book *Educated in Romance*. Note the date of this research: just after the peak of the Women's Liberation movement.[7]

I will come back to the hidden curriculum in later chapters; for the moment, I will concentrate on the formal curriculum. In almost all universities today, its main source is the research-based knowledge formation. In faculties of Arts and Sciences, and generic courses in other faculties, this knowledge formation provides almost all the formal content. The course titles tell this: Physics 201, Sociology of Migration, Introduction to Plant Genetics. Course guides often cite the research publications that underpin each lecture or tutorial.

In professional faculties such as Medicine, Engineering or Education, students learn the practical business of their future occupation, including how to make informed judgments such as diagnoses. Research-based knowledge is also used here, though organized differently as it is mingled with occupational know-how. In professional courses there is commonly a tension between theory and practice, at worst a split in the curriculum, at best a creative merging.

In either case, there are choices for the teachers to make. Universities do not take research output and feed it raw to the students. I have never seen a course, however advanced, that did that. Every curriculum is a *selection* from the archive of available knowledge. This was made very clear in the lively debates around new interdisciplinary programmes in the 1960s and 1970s, for instance at the Open University in Britain. The disorderly output of research has to be coded into an orderly form. The material has to fit into a given timetable slot, no less and no more; it has to be arranged in a sequence that can be taught and tested; a balance has to be struck between tried-and-true classics and up-to-the-minute discoveries.[8]

Though every teacher does some of this coding, it takes a spectacular form in textbooks. A successful text like Paul Samuelson's *Economics* (now in its nineteenth edition, plus translations and overseas adaptations) can sell literally millions of copies. And a popular textbook is not left lonely. Nowadays it comes online as well as in print, with a guide explaining how to teach it, a confidential suite of exam questions – helpfully telling the professor the right answers – and a website offering extra readings and video material for the students.

This may seem insulting to the professor, who is supposed to be an authority in the field! But it is highly practical for teachers in precarious employment, who have to present, at short notice, courses on subjects where they are not authorities. Therefore a textbook is highly practical for agile managers who want to mount courses, and hire or re-deploy teachers, at short notice when they see a market opportunity.

The textbookized curriculum (to coin a horrible name for a horrible phenomenon) confronts the student as a pre-determined body of information, techniques and rules. Most students are not troubled by this: they arrive at the university already familiar with pre-determined curricula. Usually only limited alternatives are offered.

Why? This is a crucial question. Samuelson's famous textbook is particularly helpful here, because economic historians have traced in detail the way it was conceived, modified and marketed. Samuelson himself was a bright young mathematical economist who was commissioned to write an introductory textbook in the 1940s. It was the heyday of Keynesian economics, when the shape of postwar economies was at stake, and the Cold War between the rival imperialisms of the United States and the Soviet Union was brewing. Samuelson worked at an elite institution, MIT, which was generously funded by the capitalists of the north-eastern United States.

Some of those businessmen took an interest in what MIT's economics department was up to, and scrutinized Samuelson's draft with unfriendly eyes, suspecting it of socialistic tendencies. Obligingly, Samuelson re-wrote the offending passages. It wasn't enough. When the book came out in 1948, he and his capitalist publisher were denounced as pro-communist, by the right-wing forces gaining strength in the United States at the time. Academic economists defended Samuelson; he re-wrote again; his department produced a book of readings balancing free-market and Keynesian positions. And so it went on, while the book sold magnificently and Samuelson went on his way to fame and fortune. What the students encountered as economics was, as the historian Yann Giraud observes, 'the result of a political negotiation'.[9]

The details of this case are dramatic, but the basic features are common. I have emphasized that curriculum is made by selection and coding. I must now add that curriculum is made in specific historical situations, by members of particular social groups, whose problems and tensions enter the process. (The political problems of US capitalism, especially conflict over the role of the state in postwar reconstruction, deeply affected Samuelson's text.) The situation in which any curriculum is written sets limits to its content, and those limits reflect power relations in the wider society. (Even if Samuelson had been a revolutionary with a bomb under his cloak, no textbook emphasizing class struggle could possibly have become a best-seller in US economics departments.)

We may speak of a *hegemonic* curriculum when university teaching accepts such limits, and the content is stabilized in teaching routines that quietly legitimate existing social relations. 'Hegemony' is a term devised by a real revolutionary, Antonio Gramsci, to describe a situation where the dominant class rules by cultural authority more than naked force. Hegemonic power operates by consent, below the radar, establishing a regime of common sense in which alternatives can hardly be imagined. Academic authority in universities often has this character, and the hegemonic curriculum in a university degree will appear to the world as simply the best and most powerful knowledge in its field. That appearance is reinforced when the hegemonic curriculum leads to credentials, opens doors to professions, and is recognized by states and corporations.

For students, the formal curriculum is decisively defined by what is tested. The US university system and the corporations that service it have evolved standardized tests for undergraduate entry (e.g. SAT, ACT) and selection for graduate programmes (e.g. GRE, TOEFL). Millions of students now sit for these tests every year. For their own courses, most departments jog along with home-made quizzes and exams, providing ritual humiliation for students and dismay for their teachers. Conventional examining normally calls out *under*-performance from students, because of hurry, test anxiety, isolation, or reliance on rote memory. With forced-choice 'objective' tests, the level of intellectual performance is lower again.[10]

In the 1960s tests and examinations fell into disrepute because of their social biases and doubtful validity. They have come back with a vengeance, not because these problems have been solved, but because policymakers and managers now require an auditing regime. Michael Power's brilliant book *The Audit Society* shows the pressure involved: organizations are required to make themselves auditable. A set of test results provides data for auditing teachers' performance, and for ranking institutions above and below each other.[11]

In a high-stakes testing regime, passing the test becomes a major goal of learning and often *the* major goal. The most efficient thing a student can do is study for the test and ignore the deeper problems raised by what she is learning. This is the hidden curriculum at work, as students become expert at exam-taking itself. I certainly did. Experience taught me that last-minute cramming gave no help. So I used to prepare by walking down, the day before the exam, to look at flowers in the Melbourne Botanic Gardens. The flowers were quite effective for controlling test anxiety, and the walk was good for my health. It didn't make me any better at Psychology or History.

There is dissent. Student movements ever since the *Córdoba Declaration* have denounced the conservatism of the university curriculum, its failure to engage with burning issues of the day. Feminism has challenged the deep bias of university disciplines in which women's experience was ignored. There is currently an outspoken movement in South Africa to de-colonize the curriculum and contest its implicit racism. In Aotearoa New Zealand, Bolivia, Ecuador and other countries, indigenous colleges and universities have been created with curricula based, at least in part, on indigenous knowledge formations.[12]

There is also tension between the hegemonic curriculum and the knowledge formation it relies on. The knowledge formation is ragged, and constantly shifting, and full of unanswered questions. The hegemonic curriculum is orderly, closed, and full of answered questions. This contradiction can be massaged. The conventional textbook pretends it is not there, marshalling facts in a deep authoritative rumble that claims to be the voice of research. But to *resolve* the contradiction, we must break with the model of pre-determined knowledge. That also means breaking with the pedagogy that is most familiar in universities.

The work of teaching

Like research, university teaching has a composite labour process. Scheduled encounters with groups of students, whether face-to-face or online, alternate with longer periods of preparation, and work such as advising and marking. The teacher is also doing emails, telephone calls, paperwork, gathering information, reading specialized literature, drafting documents, reporting online, holding committee meetings and individual discussions with colleagues. For academics in a research university, all that work alternates with research as well. The routine is irregular and – contrary to images of the ivory tower – usually done under time pressure.

To sustain this composite labour requires intricate scheduling. Young academics find it frantic at first. They gradually discover how many days it takes to write a lecture or compile a research report. No one can schedule automatically: the balance is constantly changing and the components blur. When I scan the new issue of a journal, for instance, I am looking for teaching materials. But I am also checking for ideas relevant to my current research, and noticing what might be useful to colleagues, and sometimes just storing background for all these purposes.

Like research, a great deal of teaching is collective labour. The public image may be a solo lecture by a star performer. The everyday reality is a team of technicians, administrative staff, tutors and lecturers moving in a ballet in which that lecture is only a passing moment. The know-how of *all* these workers, their day-to-day coordination, and their capacity to sustain the coordination over months and years, are what really make up mainstream university teaching.

Educationists have tried to measure whether active researchers make the best teachers. The results are muddy, but mostly suggest there is no strong correlation at the level of the individual. I am not surprised. Teaching and research compete for any worker's time and energy. Though the skill-sets overlap, they are not identical. Anyone familiar with a university can probably name a wonderful teacher who does little research, and a high-flying researcher who is dull in the classroom.[13]

The real point is not the individual correlation, but the *collective* relationship between teaching and research. A contemporary university teaches in the presence of the research-based knowledge formation, drawing on its archive for the curriculum. A programme that teaches research-based knowledge at an advanced level needs the involvement of staff with an intimate understanding of how that knowledge is made. This connection is currently at risk.

Most university teaching is designed on a simple model, closely linked with the hegemonic curriculum. It assumes that the pupil is defined by lack of knowledge and the teacher by fullness of knowledge. Educationists sardonically call this 'empty-vessel' pedagogy: the teacher's job is to pour the divine fluid of knowledge into the pupil's head, and then measure the level it has reached. The great Brazilian educator Paulo Freire tweaked the metaphor and called it the 'banking' concept of education, with the teacher making little deposits of knowledge which the students patiently receive, file and store.[14]

To put it more plainly, content is decided in advance, and the process is treated as knowledge transfer. The standard practices for doing this in universities are lectures, textbooks, course guides, prescribed readings, demonstrations, pre-planned laboratory or practical exercises, pre-planned group discussions, quizzes and exams.

The classic university technique is the lecture, and I want to spend a moment considering this as an educational device. The distinguishing feature of university architecture is the lecture hall or theatre. This is basically a container for empty-vessel pedagogy on a grand scale. I have spent a lot of time in such theatres, addressing 50 to 500 people at a time, on one terrifying occasion about 3000. Each time I felt I should apologise for the mistake that brought us together in such a place.

A lecture typically contains a few principles, which the course plan requires to be covered in that hour, plus a number of illustrations or cases. A really skilled performer can make the hour gripping – a celebrity lecturer such as Richard Feynman, the physicist I quoted in Chapter 1. But it is the basic logic of the lecture that determines how it works in mass higher education. The logic is made visible by the theatre's floor-plan, placing the lecturer at the focus of the room and providing benches or fixed seats for the students. The students' capacities for action are hemmed in, their interaction is sharply restricted, a norm of passivity is forced upon them. It is not surprising when they take refuge in their Facebook, Twitter or Instagram accounts. If the speaker calls for discussion, the usual result is a spatter of unrelated questions from random individuals.

Students' notes from a lecture are embarrassing for any lecturer to read. As a method of knowledge transfer, this is a little better than sneezing in Morse code, but not much. Yet there is one thing that can always be said in its favour. Lecturing is cheap.

It is getting cheaper, too, as lectures go online. Corporate-style managements are now recording lectures given by their academic staff and claiming copyright in them. In 2012 the MOOC model made a splash. It greatly excited management consultants, who declared MOOCs would render the business model of the traditional university obsolete. By 2015 there were already more than 4000 of them, claiming 35 million students enrolled. Though there have been attempts to make MOOCs more interactive, they are mainly ways of getting lectures out to much larger numbers of students via the Web. The staggering drop-out rate – usually over 90 per cent – suggests how excited the students become.[15]

Students also attend tutorials or sections, many courses have laboratory or field sessions, and up-to-the-minute universities also have online chat groups on closed websites. These are activities intended to help students grasp the pre-determined content, and keep up their morale. They rarely yield sustained control over learning, and they rarely challenge the social limits embedded in the hegemonic curriculum.

Consider, for instance, the famous 'case' method in the Harvard MBA, 'a profound educational innovation' according to the modest website of the Harvard Business School. Teams of students are given well-documented problems, and asked to develop solutions. There is scope for student creativity here. But what are these problems? Dilemmas experienced by leading corporations, NGOs and governments in the market economy. Basically, the students are learning techniques for fiercer competition within the taken-for-granted world of capitalism.[16]

Once we get beyond the hegemonic curriculum and the idea of knowledge transfer, a subversive logic in higher education emerges. Teaching can create conditions for the students to transform their own capacities. The great Soviet psychologist Lev Vygotsky proposed the idea of a 'zone of proximal development' in learning, the tasks just beyond a pupil's current capacity, where educational intervention and peer-group support can be effective. This led in later educational thought to the idea of teaching as providing 'scaffolding' for students' learning. It is a helpful idea. If there is one thing vital in university teaching, it is the teacher's capacity to work out the next move in a complex intellectual task, and give students practical help to make it. This is the basic role of the teacher when the curriculum is *not* pre-determined.[17]

It is exceptionally clear at the most advanced level of teaching – supervising a PhD thesis. There is little possibility of knowledge transfer in the researchable zone where knowledge itself is being created. But there is a great deal that supervisors can do as students move into that dangerous zone. They can give help ranging from morning-coffee dialogues on subtle problems of theory, to pure emotional support, to stealing copy paper for the student from the departmental cupboard.[18]

The principle applies in undergraduate teaching too. To take the next steps in a learning process they have designed themselves, students may need to clarify some concept, get wider information, learn some technique, or evaluate their own work. I am not offering blueprints, but a couple of examples may help.

At Macquarie University I was involved one year in a course on the sociology of gender, that was organized as a set of self-managed research groups. One of the groups decided to research men and masculinity, using focussed interviews. All members of this group were women. My role as teacher was not to choose the project, that was part of their learning. Rather, it was to help the students take each next step once they had defined their direction: focus the problem, develop the method, divide the tasks, find the (then slender) research literature, overcome difficulties in fieldwork, interpret what they discovered, and communicate their findings. It was a gripping experience; I think it was the first research on that subject that anyone in the country had done.

A more recent example is a geography course run by Jen Bagelman, in a Canadian university which had been awarded top marks in a league table for food sustainability. The course dug behind this award. The students knew the university was built on land that had never been ceded by indigenous peoples. They began researching the campus foodscape within this history of colonial displacement. They reported their findings in the form of zines, and they proposed changes in the university's food supply and distribution. This course was a small unit, but it managed to combine student initiative, postcolonial perspectives, environmental knowledge, alternative media, and practical applications.[19]

Learning with excitement and with consequences – the metaphor of 'catching fire' is barely adequate for this creative process – need not be an elite experience at all. It can happen in a service course in statistics, it can happen in a vocational course, and it should happen in all of them.

A democratic approach to curriculum does not make teaching obsolete, but changes its logic. The teacher no longer stands over the students as the Missionary from the Republic of Knowledge. The teacher is on both sides of the relationship, working for the students as well as for the republic. To work for the students, to support the next step they need to make and the next step after that, demands that the teacher learns to know them – as well as having background research-based knowledge and taking a hand in producing new knowledge. This takes time, but it matters a great deal. Learning *by the teacher* is a central part of a democratic educational process. It is especially important when the students are from social groups new in universities – which is now happening on a tremendous scale with the worldwide expansion of the university system.

We should think of the teacher as midwife, as scaffold-builder, as experimenter, as learner, and sometimes as a guard protecting the space in which groups of students are doing the work of learning. That may seem a less dignified role. You cannot wear a robe and mortarboard while hammering scaffolds or helping with a difficult birth. But it is an immensely demanding, skilled, and rewarding role. And what it lacks in dignity it gains in relevance. We can have a model for teaching that treats the university as a democratic workplace – for *all* its workers – pursuing democratic purposes for the whole society.

Chapter 3

The collective intellectual: university workers

Intellectuals

According to classic theories, intellectuals should be ruling the world. A century and a half ago, Auguste Comte hailed 'savants' as bearers of social progress, in alliance with women and workers. Mikhail Bakunin, who was Karl Marx's great rival in the European left, made an uncanny prediction that socialist savants would try to rule over the workers. Lenin and Stalin made this prediction come true. Julien Benda's 1928 best-seller *The Treason of the Intellectuals* argued urgently for French intellectuals to keep their distance from the corrupting world of political emotion. Karl Mannheim, whose *Ideology and Utopia* caused a stir in Germany the following year, saw a third way, where independent intellectuals might create a scientific politics. This was one of the ideas behind the European welfare state.

The next generation began to picture intellectuals as a 'new class'. To dissidents analysing communist regimes, Lenin's vanguard appeared as the core of a new power structure. In the capitalist world, a strategic role for the bearers of knowledge seemed to be required by giant corporations with complex finance and planning needs, by new technologies such as nuclear weapons, and by government involvement in the economy. The economist John Kenneth Galbraith argued this, calling knowledge workers 'the technostructure'. An influential book by the sociologist Alvin Gouldner, *The Future of Intellectuals and the Rise of the New Class*, saw higher education and professions as the basis of a 'culture of critical discourse'. Others too, impressed with the student movement and counter-culture of the 1960s, saw intellectuals as opposed to the power of capital, or at least leading a new middle class.

The idea of an intelligentsia as a new elite with its own culture lived on. Richard Florida in *The Rise of the Creative Class* pictured a culture of individuality and creativity that was driving urban prosperity. New-right publicists produced a hostile version of this idea, in polemics against Ivy-educated coastal elites indifferent to the ordinary working man. This version has been rolled out in the United States by the Tea Party and the Trump administration, and in Europe by anti-EU populism such as the Brexit campaign. Meanwhile new-left theorists have looked to 'immaterial labour' in the current economy (to use the language of Hardt and Negri's *Empire*) for new strategies of revolution.[1]

All this makes a great story; it is a pity it is wrong. The new class, on close inspection, does not seem very new, nor much like a class. Its power is hard to define, and its critical culture is curiously elusive. The story line is strikingly Eurocentric: intellectuals as influential as Mahatma Gandhi and Sayed Jamal al-Din al-Afghani are overlooked. And it is hard to find women in this narrative, except as the angelic helpmeets of Monsieur Comte's lively imagination.

We need to come closer to the ground. In the first two chapters of this book I talked about the intellectual labour of universities, both research and education, as a collective undertaking. To understand universities we need to understand the workforce who do this labour, who are collectively the modern intellectual. This workforce is large, international, and still growing. It is also intricately divided. In this chapter I will focus on the situation inside universities, especially how university workers make universities function, and the changing conditions of their work.[2]

Though current debates about university work focus strongly on academics, at least half the workers are *not* academics. Judy Szekeres has rightly called attention to 'the invisible workers' of universities, who are so often disregarded that the group does not even have an agreed name. I have heard them called non-academic staff, support personnel, professional workers, administrative staff, general staff, or just 'staff'. Given their importance in making the university operate as an organization, I will call them the operations workers. They are as much part of the collective intellectual as academics are.

Academic workers and operations workers are not entirely distinct. Julia Whitchurch speaks of blurred boundaries and the emergence of 'third space' professionals in universities. There are certainly such blended roles, and they dramatize the connectedness of different forms of labour in universities. Mostly, however, academic and operations workers are employed under different conditions, with different career paths, pay scales and job titles.[3]

Operations workers

Universities do not publish directories of their operations workers, and there is not a great deal of research about them, so information in the public domain is limited. Here is a rough list of the groups usually present on a university campus:

- clerical workers, front office staff, personal assistants
- maintenance trades (electricians, carpenters, etc.), grounds staff
- janitors/building attendants
- cleaners

- construction workers of all kinds (when new facilities are going up)
- campus police, security workers
- transport workers
- computing and telecommunications staff
- laboratory technicians and other technical workers
- librarians, curators, archivists
- accountants, purchasing officers and other finance staff
- administrators of programmes and units (departments, schools, etc.)
- services to management (lawyers, architects, personnel, advertising, etc.)
- services to students (catering, health, counselling, accommodation, etc.)
- managers.

Other groups of workers may arrive when a university has a specialized role. For instance the Open University in England, when setting up for distance education, hired artists, editors, publishers, printers, broadcast producers and specialized course assistants.[4]

The balance among groups changes over time. Recently the number of librarians has declined while the number of computer staff has risen. The upper-level managers are a unique group in most ways, including their pay packets, and I will tell their story in Chapter 6.

What leaps out from this list is the variety of the work being done, to make a university function. Some is manual labour (grounds staff, security, the trades), some is certified professional work (accountants, lawyers, counsellors). Some involves specialized skills (computing staff, electricians, librarians), rather more involves generic skills of office work and administration. Operations workers bring different forms of knowledge into the university. There is nothing unusual here: divisions of labour along these lines are found in most large organizations.

There is also variety in the labour process, i.e. the way work is organized. Some is episodic. Maintenance workers and some of the computing staff are called to deal with problems as they arise – a leaking window, a frozen computer – and their work takes them irregularly around the campus. Especially at upper levels of the organization, work may be organized on a project basis. Other parts of the work have a more regular flow. Clerical staff, accountants, building attendants or librarians usually work in a particular space and stay there continuously. Though most of the operations staff use generic equipment like personal computers, telephones and cars, laboratory technicians use – or even make – highly specialized tools and equipment.

There could be, then, a severe fragmentation within university work. But there are many ways that the groups of workers link with each other. Shared work spaces and daily cooperation can create strong social ties. The flows of the composite labour of research and teaching, and the maintenance of the organization, are constantly linking and re-linking different groups of workers.

To mount an undergraduate course, for instance, the lecturer or professor will have to book rooms with the administrators in charge of timetables. The rooms are prepared by cleaners, and the equipment is maintained by tradespeople. Course guides have to be printed and distributed by office staff, or mounted online with the help of ICT staff. Students may enrol for the course at the services desk, and when they cannot find the room will get directions from building attendants. The lecturer will liaise with personnel officers in appointing casual tutors (adjunct teaching assistants), and with finance officers in getting the tutors paid their pittances. Textbooks and supplementary reading will be arranged by librarians. Students will prepare for exams with the aid of cafeteria workers on the coffee machines, and recover with the aid of counsellors. All this has to happen for every course, in every department, in every quarter, term or semester.[5]

Equally complex coordination by the operations staff is involved in making any research project happen, over the years that a research grant might last. The crucial point is the way different workers pick up the thread of an organizational process, work on it with their own skills and knowledge, and send the process forward. They do this again and again, for the hundreds of threads that have to be woven together to produce educational and research results.

This constant, active interweaving, which makes up the daily life of the university workforce, is not like the repetitive labour of mass production. It depends on vocational skills and knowledge, but it also depends very heavily on *situational* knowledge. This is the organizational know-how about where the task is heading, what its next steps are, what the likely problems are, and who else has to become involved.

Here is an account by one operations worker of how her job evolved over years:

> It was a combination of relief receptionist and … entering data … [I also] just started using the old SE/30 Macs and a lot of people weren't familiar with using them so then I sort of found niches where I could support people to learn applications or support people with networking. I kind of evolved into lots of different things but I was sort of then doing a bit of database design because I picked up those skills and that sort of stuff and evolved into a role where I was working exclusively with special needs students. It wasn't a role that existed when I started but then I kind of evolved into it …
>
> Then that job in itself also evolved. So I was sort of looking after the note takers, the interpreters and developed a database to manage them in terms of looking at what students need and what sort of support and then matching and booking people for the timetables and that sort of stuff. And also payment and that kind of thing. I mean, the manager still approved payment but I still managed time sheets and things and stuff.[6]

This story refers to a particular Australian university and a particular moment in technology. But it nicely shows the constant interweaving of tasks, the linking with different groups of workers and students, and the sheer creativity of operations staff.

In the universities I know best, organizational know-how used to be embodied in the department secretary. The secretary was not academically qualified herself, but was a fountain of information about the university, its rules and its people. She was skilled in corralling professors, office workers and tradesmen, she could make things happen on time and in correct form. She knew when care work needed to be done: advising anxious students and frazzled junior lecturers, heading off conflicts and crises. When my academic career began, department secretaries were the most important people in making the university function day by day. When my career ended, the role had almost disappeared.

That was a particular case of a more general issue: how the disparate and potentially fragmented work of a university is held together. It is held together informally *from below*, by the organizational know-how of the operations staff, and their ability to improvise and innovate. They create connections and find solutions to move a process forward, whether the process is enrolling students, enabling research, or getting people paid. And then they improvise again, with adjustments, as the next task comes through.

This coordination-from-below links the operations staff to the research-based knowledge formation and to teaching. Which is to say, it makes a university possible. All the strategic plans would be dust in the wind if this unsung work of coordination were not being done every working day.

These are realities, but we cannot be romantic about them. Coordination can be difficult, and constantly has to cross boundaries and levels. Administrators can be alienated or obstructive. Universities have normally been hierarchical places. Charles Crothers, in a study of one university department in Aotearoa New Zealand, observes:

> There must be few small-scale social units in a capitalist society where such an extraordinary range of inequalities jostles cheek-by-jowl within a group of people ostensibly carrying out the same sort of activities.[7]

University staffing reflects familiar class, gender and racial inequalities. The operations staff are generally lower-paid than the academics. In Australia in 2010, their average salary was 80 per cent of the average academic salary – lower again, for non-managerial staff. Again taking the case of Australia, a majority are women: 66 per cent of all the operations staff in 2014. But women are a minority in the upper reaches of the pay scale, and that tells an old story of interrupted careers, dead-end jobs, lower qualifications, and men's structural privilege. In a survey across 36 Australian universities in 2006–7, of all operations staff who did *not* have a university qualification, 84 per cent were women. These patterns are not unique to Australia.[8]

Middle-class men predominate at the management and professional levels; working-class men in the grounds staff, the security personnel and the tradespeople. In countries where social class advantage is interwoven with racial exclusion, operations staff are more likely to be Black while academic and managerial staff are more likely to be White. For most of the operations staff, there has been nothing one could call a career. Often the only way to advance would be to resign and move to another job entirely. However, this issue has been taken up by unions, and for some groups, including finance officers and librarians, promotion pathways have been built.

Operations workers are not a privileged new class, but they have some good reasons for working in universities. Universities are relatively safe places to work, though they are also sites of harassment. Until recently they offered good job security and only moderate workplace stress. Many in the operations staff value the institution. They like working with students, and appreciate working for the public good, so they take pride in working for a university. I have heard this said on the picket line, in the coffee shop, and in everyday work.

All these things are subject to change. A notable study of German universities by Georg Krücken and colleagues showed an expansion of higher management and a contraction of lower-grade operations staff due to 'restructuring and outsourcing'. That seems a common pattern internationally. Some areas of operations have expanded: computing, marketing, research administration, compliance, university 'advancement' (a euphemism for fundraising), and student services. Jobs at departmental level, close to the academics, have been reduced. There has been a tendency to centralize the operations staff directly under the control of top management. Plainly there is a pattern here.[9]

One change needs particular attention, the 'outsourcing' of operations work. With outsourcing the work may still be done on campus, but the university is not legally the employer. The university management has a contract with another company, which employs the labour and supplies the service. The labour costs will be smaller, the workers' benefits fewer, and union membership lower; that is the point of outsourcing. With this move, part of the university's actual workforce vanishes from the statistics, which do not count contractors as university employees.

I first noticed this process when our university printery was abolished, so departments had to buy their printing work from outside suppliers. Outsourcing has now spread to ICT, grounds work, security, cleaning, financial records, building maintenance, and there is no logical reason to stop there. Under pressure from unions and students, the University of Cape Town in South Africa recently reversed its policy of outsourcing, but this is still an exceptional case.[10]

Outsourcing is a really important, and little-discussed, change in universities. It undermines operations workers' situational knowledge. The outsourced workers are not at the university long-term, and have no role in its decision-making. Outsourcing undermines the grassroots coordination of the labour process, since the remaining university staff cannot easily get to know the outsourced workers, either. Outsourcing looks great from a management finance point of view. But it weakens the knowledge resources on which a university operates.

Academic workers

There is a flood of writing about academic life: novels, plays, ethnographies, surveys, manifestos, autobiographies and satires. There are even murder-mystery series with an academic hero or heroine, spilling scholarly quotations all over the clues. Absent-minded professors proliferate in popular cartoons, though sometimes a little sinister, scrawling on a blackboard (always a blackboard!) the formula for a new kind of radioactivity.

The academic staff generally come from more privileged backgrounds than the operations staff, in terms of class and race. Recruitment to academic work depends heavily on success in school and university examinations, so mirrors the social biases built into the hegemonic curriculum. Socially marginalized groups – peasants, Untouchables, indigenous people, Latinos, Blacks, recent migrants, refugees – are severely under-represented. In Australia, a country with massive and diverse immigration in the last two generations, the academic workforce remains overwhelmingly White, Anglo and upper middle class in background.

When my great-aunts Maud and Rita arrived as students at the University of Melbourne in the 1880s and 1890s, all their professors were men. That university waited until 1975 – by then my great-aunts had died in old age – to make its first appointment of a woman to a full professorship, the pathologist Priscilla Kincaid-Smith. The vice-chancellor of a new Canadian university in the 1960s, describing his recruitment strategy, unconsciously expressed the prevailing attitude: 'Good men attract other good men.' Women, barred from elite networks, given insecure jobs, spilled out of the promotion pipeline, and held back by radically unequal divisions of labour at home, have fought long and hard for access. The fight is still going on. Women are currently a majority of students, but only one-fifth of full professors, in Australia. Women in fields like physics and biomedical science still run up against boys' clubs and masculinized cultures.[11]

Close-focus research has laid emphasis on disciplinary differences within the academic workforce. That was the main theme of Tony Becher's much-cited book *Academic Tribes and Territories*. If the reader can forgive the colonialist idea that cultural difference signals a 'tribe', and the fact that Mr Becher mostly forgot to interview women, this study did show different styles of work between academic disciplines.[12] Some disciplines publish books, others articles; some do lab work, others fieldwork; some do research as individuals, others in teams. Some disciplines are connected with professions outside the university, others are not. Arts and Social Sciences are notoriously more to the left than Engineering or Medicine, and worse dressed than Law.

Yet when soberly viewed, it is impossible to see these differences as separate cultures in any ethnographic sense. In industrial terms they are simply variations on a shared model of production and distribution. In all university disciplines, the dominant features of knowledge work are the composite labour processes described in Chapters 1 and 2. In research universities there has been a strong sense that the academic job *is* the combination of teaching, research and service.

This implies a problem of coordination within the job. Balances have to be struck every day between very different tasks, as I mentioned for teaching. The endless balancing reflects the traditionally craft-like character of academic work, where the experienced worker has control over the direction and pace of the work, and assessment of quality is mainly in the hands of the workforce itself.[13]

Autonomy is one of the most valued features of academic jobs. In a wide sense, autonomy means scope to negotiate one's own balances between the different elements of the labour process. In a narrower sense, it means the right to independent judgment in one's own area of research or teaching, the famous principle of 'academic freedom'.

Without that kind of autonomy, research can be forced down blind alleys. That happened from the 1920s in the Soviet Union, when the agronomist Trofim Lysenko came up with optimistic ideas that suited the regime's urgent political needs at a time of agricultural collapse. Belief in the easy mutability of crop species, and therefore in agricultural miracles, became the only theory that would keep a Soviet biologist safe from the secret police. Lysenko was not a charlatan, but he was not a good researcher either. He was given political power to enforce a scientific error, and used it.

That was a striking, but historically rare, event. Governments do not usually try to prescribe the outcomes of research. They more often try to silence embarrassing researchers. That has been happening in recent years about climate change. Right-wing governments in Canada and Australia, committed to the oil, gas and coal industries, have tried to hamper or discredit environmental science. When the Trump administration came to power in the United States it promptly did the same, forbidding the publication of scientific findings on government websites. Within a year it was trying to censor medical research too.

In the 1950s suspected communists were purged from US universities. That wasn't about nuclear secrets – a prominent target, Alex Novikoff, was a cell biologist – but about displays of 'loyalty'. Political attacks on academics continue. In Australia, the right-wing Murdoch newspapers targeted a colleague of mine in media studies at the University of Sydney in 2014; and the ultra-conservative faction of the government parties targeted sexuality researchers at La Trobe University in 2016. There is currently an international campaign, led by fundamentalists both Protestant and Catholic, against so-called 'gender theory'. In Turkey, more than 5000 academics are said to have been arrested or thrown out of their jobs by the Erdoğan government since the failed military coup of 2016.[14]

Vice-chancellors, rectors and presidents know they should defend academic freedom against outside attacks, and sometimes they do. But there is also a running fight *inside* universities about the autonomy of academic workers. As Mats Alvesson shows in his excellent book on knowledge-intensive firms, managers have a control problem even in the corporate world. Intellectual workers prefer non-hierarchical workplaces, claim professional autonomy, have widespread communication links, and need flexibility.[15] University managers have now gained the upper hand in this contest, a key move being the installation of online systems which also serve as control mechanisms. I will come back to this issue in Chapter 6.

There has been another major change in academic employment, the growth of untenured, part-time or fixed-term jobs. Universities have long made use of untenured demonstrators, teaching assistants, assistant professors or *Dozenten*, at the start of an academic career. Managers did not need to set up a new structure: they simply arranged budgets and job specifications in ways that made career progression stall. A highly trained workforce, loaded with doctorates, has swelled at an early point in the career pipeline.

Indeed we could say that this pipeline hardly exists any more. Much of the academic labour force has become permanently insecure. Joseph Schwartz, surveying the academic job scene in the United States, notes that between 1976 and 2011, the numbers of full-time tenured or tenure-track faculty grew by 23 per cent, while the number of full-time *non*-tenure-track faculty grew by 259 per cent and part-time faculty (adjuncts) grew by 286 per cent! He sums up the change pithily:

> [T]here are more university faculty today than ever before; but only thirty percent of them have tenured jobs or positions eligible for tenure, versus seventy percent in the early 1970s.

A similar change has occurred in Australia. Currently around 40 per cent of the academic workers here are employed on a temporary basis, around double the rate in the Australian economy as a whole. I say 'around', because governments and university managements make it difficult to find the details. They prefer to report the 'full-time equivalent' rate, which is about 22 per cent, since most casuals are part-time. That looks better. It still means that around 70 per cent of the undergraduate teaching is done by insecure labour. The universities definitely do not advertise that.[16]

This has immediate consequences for the quality of teaching as well as career progress and job satisfaction. Casual staff are not involved in course planning, so they teach courses they have not designed. They are rarely offered staff development to improve their skills. They usually have no offices for meeting students – at best a hot desk, and at worst a coffee shop or their mobile telephone.

This also changes the work of tenured staff. Rather than mentoring new recruits to the profession, they find themselves working as overseers: finding, hiring and managing a crew of untenured staff. This is now usual in generalist courses with large enrolments, which are cheaper to teach and administer than an array of small specialized courses. Current trends are splitting academic labour into a primary and a secondary workforce, with a hierarchical relation between them.

Casualized teachers are not funded to do research, even though many of them have a PhD – which is a research, not a teaching, qualification. It is difficult to create a research agenda if you have no funding, no job stability, and no office. Casualization thus tends to split teaching from research. This is also happening in tenured jobs: a growing number of academics are being appointed as research-only or teaching-only. In management-consultant speak, this is 'unbundling' the academic role.[17]

If we look at higher education as a whole, the effect is magnified. Except for ruling-class institutions like Stanford and Yale, most private universities are effectively teaching-only. That is where most of the profit comes from, and that is where most of the recent global growth of universities has been. The implications of dividing research from teaching are not much discussed in public, they are too embarrassing. There are potentially very large consequences.[18]

Sustainability crisis

Any industry has to sustain its labour force and its organizations over time. The workers need adequate training and income, and the industry needs new workers from generation to generation. Adam Smith understood this well: he called paying a decent wage a matter of 'common humanity'.[19]

Universities in rich countries, until fairly recently, assumed that sustaining the sector would be easy. Operations staff as well as academics were expected to be long-term employees, who would learn on the job the skills and organizational know-how they did not have at entry. Craftsmen and typists got their tickets at the technical college down the road. Academics were trained by the university system itself. The modern PhD was invented in the United States for this purpose. A group of elite universities with doctoral programmes produced each others' future workers, plus a large surplus who went out quietly to the non-elite university and college sector. There is a beautiful account of this process in John Williams' novel *Stoner*, a neglected classic of academic life.[20]

That was the steady-state solution. It also served for periods of expansion, as long as the organizational model of the university was stable. More operations staff could be recruited from the labour market outside. For academic staff, the intake to higher degrees could be increased and the time between steps shortened. My generation started in a period of expansion, and I was offered a job with tenure the moment I had a PhD. That is inconceivable now, because the steady-state model has broken down.

What universities face in this generation is not material decline – globally, higher education has been briskly expanding. Yet there is malaise in the system. Twenty years ago, Sandra Acker and Grace Feuerverger published a close-focus study of women professors of education in Canada, a group of committed and successful academics who should have been happy. They turned out to be overworked, anxious, even distressed. The researchers called their paper 'Doing good and feeling bad', and they were prophetic. The changes discussed in this chapter have produced a heavy weight of 'feeling bad' across the workforce.[21]

This is intense among the casualized teachers. Highly trained academic workers live, year after year, on erratic incomes cobbled together from an assortment of temporary contracts. In Chile, the first country in the world to turn neoliberal – at the point of a bayonet – they have a name for this. Casualized teachers who rush from university to university to teach different classes are called 'Taxi Professors'. I remember one casualized teacher, during the 2013 strike at Sydney, describing this situation as 'a life of humiliation', having to beg for work. Megan Kimber and Lisa Ehrich speak of a 'lost generation' of academic staff.[22]

In a recent paper George Morgan and Julian Wood describe the experience of two casualized workers in close focus, and I will summarize one of the stories. Di is 32 and has worked as a casual tutor in her faculty since joining it as a PhD student seven years ago. She is a migrant, but from an English-speaking country, and is no cultural outsider. She finished the PhD but has not managed to convert much of it into publications nor obtain a post-doctoral grant or a secure job. Sometimes she seems to regret the effort: *I look at it, sitting in the drawer and think 'why did I bother?'* She is sceptical of the honesty and compassion of the senior staff, blaming them for failing to mentor her, and just using her to fill gaps in their tutoring workforce. On the other hand she speculates that tenured academics have a *nice life* and she feels the loss of an idealized academic community.

Di questions her status and self-worth a lot, and her situation is hardly sustainable in the long run. Scale this up, and you get a sense of what is happening at system level. Even in rich countries a growing proportion of the academic workforce now live in precarious conditions, lacking healthcare and secure housing, under stress and with no long-term career prospects.[23]

Outsourcing has had a bigger impact on the operations staff, weakening the coordination-from-below and the care work on which universities have relied. David Pick, Stephen Teo and Melissa Young note that the new managerial policies in Australia 'have produced unintended human costs' for operations staff, including rising insecurity and stress, less job satisfaction, and few chances to participate in workplace decisions. To put that more bluntly, operations staff get pushed around. In a large British study, M. Y. Tytherleigh and colleagues found widespread occupational stress across the higher education workforce, with the strongest stressor being job insecurity. They note, in mild academic prose, that staff were 'particularly concerned by the lack of value and trust they perceived from their organizations'. One could also put that more bluntly.[24]

In most postcolonial countries there is less boasting about quality, and a longer history of material struggle. When small numbers of universities were founded by postcolonial states, the salaries and conditions of the workforce could be quite good in local terms. In some countries, such as Brazil, secure employment was guaranteed by achieving civil service status. Over time, as state investment in the sector stagnated or declined, relative salaries for academics seem to have declined, and the story for operations staff is not likely to be different. Philip Altbach, one of the leading researchers on higher education and no panic-monger, observed 20 years ago that growing insecurity and reduced circumstances for academics were already worldwide.[25]

When full-time academic salaries are inadequate, moonlighting becomes common and less care and commitment is invested in the university. Operations staff salaries may not be enough to guarantee that the fabric and services of a university are well maintained. Especially in the regional and private universities where most growth in the system has occurred, the result can be poor morale among staff and poor physical conditions for both staff and students. Yet the students here are the most likely to be first-in-family to attend university, and the least skilled in international languages. As a group they need *more* resources for learning than other students, not less.[26]

Crises have erupted in several countries. In India in 2009–14, no less than 44 'deemed universities' were investigated and failed the criteria, while the gold rush to open private universities produced a series of fraud scandals and corporate smashes. In South Africa, trust in universities by many Black students, and at least some Black staff, collapsed and some universities were forced to shut down in 2015–16. Jonathan Jansen gives a vivid picture in his recent book *As by Fire: The End of the South African University*, attributing the crisis to under-funding by government and a disruptive student movement – a vice-chancellor's perspective. In Britain, the largest strike movement in the university sector's history broke out in 2018, over sharp cuts in the sector's pension fund.[27]

The details of conflict vary, but the evidence of systems under stress is clear. In the transformation of universities into an expanding and profitable global industry, damage has been done to the credibility of universities and to their working as organizations. In most parts of the world, universities are not at breakdown point. But the current solutions are temporary, the illusions are many, and underneath there seems to be a gathering crisis of sustainability for the universities and their workforce.

Chapter 4

The global economy of knowledge

The research-based knowledge formation, which underpins most of the university curriculum, is embedded in an economy of knowledge – a system of production, distribution and exchange – as well as an economy of goods and money.

Like the material economy, the economy of knowledge is worldwide and highly unequal. North America and western Europe have most of the celebrity researchers, top research institutes, leading journals and research funds, while European languages dominate academic publishing. It is not surprising that in Africa, the Islamic world and East Asia, the research-based knowledge formation is often called 'Western science'. That is a common view in Europe and North America too, where it is comfortably assumed that 'the West' invented modern knowledge, and then gifted it to the rest of the world.

In fact, the knowledge economy in which the research-based formation emerged is not so much Western as Imperial. The wider world played a crucial role in its history from the beginning. Even the numbers we count with are known as Arabic numerals! The real story is more interesting than usually imagined, and highly relevant to the future of universities.[1]

Imperial science

The best starting-point for understanding the knowledge economy is the philosopher Paulin Hountondji's brilliant essay 'Recentring Africa'. This is the opening chapter in *Endogenous Knowledge*, a collection of West African studies of science and technology, published in French in 1994 and English in 1997. Hountondji's work is not well known outside Africa, and this essay is rarely cited in international science and technology studies or even postcolonial studies. Why? Because it was not published by Harvard or Oxford, but in Dakar, the capital of Senegal, by the African social science organization CODESRIA.[2]

The expansion of European overseas power, from the sixteenth century on, created a global trade in knowledge alongside the trade in spices, silver, sugar, cotton and slaves. Vast amounts of data flowed to the metropole and went into the making of botany, zoology, astronomy, geology, oceanography, climatology, ethnography, sociology, linguistics, archaeology, palaeontology, and more. The data were collected by explorers and travellers, missionaries, military officers and colonial officials, and increasingly by professionals who travelled to the colonized world simply to collect data. Famous figures in the history of science went on these expeditions, including Alexander von Humboldt, Thomas Huxley, and most notable of all, the founder of evolutionary biology. Charles Darwin's *Journal of Researches into the Natural History and Geology of the Countries Visited during the Voyage of H.M.S. 'Beagle' Round the World* was not only a best-selling travel book but also a striking demonstration of the coloniality of knowledge.[3]

Modern botanical classification derives from the work of Carl von Linné (Linnaeus) in eighteenth-century Sweden. Linnaeus himself travelled as a young man to the Swedish colony in the far north, Lapland, collecting plants. But for much of his career he worked at the University of Uppsala on specimens brought back from the wider colonial world, especially by a team of advanced students, whom he jokingly called his 'Apostles'. These men travelled the world collecting, going to North and South America, Africa, Asia, even across the Pacific with Lieutenant Cook. The two botanists aboard Cook's ship *Endeavour*, Banks and Solander, were so excited at what they found in the south-west Pacific that Cook named the landing-place 'Botany Bay'.

The process became routine as the European university system expanded into the colonies. Witness the career of Edgeworth David, a young Welsh intellectual who came out to the colony of New South Wales in the 1880s as an official geologist. He soon discovered profitable tin and coal fields in areas recently occupied by indigenous communities. He was then appointed professor at the University of Sydney, and had an adventurous scientific career. He mapped the geology of Australia, drilled on coral islands in the Pacific, and led an extremely cold excursion to the South Magnetic Pole in Antarctica. He was made a Fellow of the Royal Society in England for his coral island work. He was eventually knighted for supervising the mines that blew up Germans on the Western Front during the Great War.[4]

A crucial fact in the history of the knowledge economy is that the circulation of knowledge between cultures and regions – which had been going on throughout history – was restructured by empire as an unequal global division of labour. While the colonies became a vast data mine, the imperial metropole (to use the French term for the colonizing centre) became the main site where data were accumulated, classified, theorized and published. This business was handled in the scientific societies, universities, botanic gardens, museums, research institutes and publishing houses of London, Paris and eventually Boston and New York.

In effect, the labour of research was divided geographically and socially, separating data collection, the encounter with materials, from theory and interpretation, the work of patterning. Further, in the laboratories and lecture halls of the metropole, research-based knowledge was turned into applied sciences or technologies, such as engineering, pharmaceuticals, medicine, agronomy, and geological mapping. In this form, knowledge was re-exported to the colonized world, and applied in colonial administration, mining and plantation economies.

As Hountondji points out, this division of labour in research outlasted the European empires, and it structures the economy of knowledge today. It has of course changed in detail. Geoscience now uses satellites and remote sensing devices, and does not need an Alexander von Humboldt scrambling up a volcano in Ecuador and measuring the air pressure (as he did in 1802, thinking he was among the highest mountains in the world). Almost all of the big quantitative models central to current climate science, which need huge computing power, are maintained in the global North; the only one in a developing country is in China. Much of the data they crunch, however, comes from the South.

Central in the knowledge economy today are the famous institutions of the global metropole. They are the elite universities such as MIT, Harvard and Cambridge, and the research institutes such as CERN, the European Centre for Nuclear Research, operating the Large Hadron Collider that found the Higgs boson; and CDC, the US Centers for Disease Control that form the world centre of biomedical research and have been crucial in the HIV/AIDS epidemic. These centres do not work in isolation. They rely on a larger mass of universities, databanks, foundations and research centres, literally thousands of institutions, supported by the wealth of European and North American society.

Universities in other regions generally follow US and European definitions of disciplines, research methods and forms of publication; their curricula and textbooks are often modelled on those in Northern universities. When the Chinese government decided to rebuild a university system after the Cultural Revolution, this is exactly what they did. They sent teams of academics and a stream of graduate students to the United States, and adapted what they found there. The first global 'league table' of universities, the Shanghai index, was a by-product of this effort.[5]

In order to participate in this global economy, researchers in the periphery must become competent in the theories and methods current in the global metropole. Their careers depend on it. Ideally they will get a PhD from a European or North American university, and publish papers in the top journals in their field, almost all of which are edited in the metropole. Here is an example from Harold, a climate scientist in South Africa whom we interviewed in the project mentioned earlier. He speaks bluntly about how he broadcasts his work:

> We weren't going for African journals because they are just not high-profile enough, to be honest. So you want to be publishing either in the leading specialist journals, which are like *Journal of Climate* and *Journal of Geophysical Research*, or if you're lucky, in *Nature* or *Science* … that's the strategy. When one's doing global-scale work, I didn't see the point of publishing in South African journals.[6]

Hountondji calls this approach 'extraversion'. Others have called it academic dependency. Hountondji's term is better, because it indicates not only accepting intellectual authority from the metropole, but also that this is an *active* response, a way of participating in the economy of knowledge. The response concerns the practical details of research, teaching, and academic careers, as well as conceptual frameworks.

Extraversion is entirely familiar to me. For many years I based my research about Australian society on theories from Europe and North America. I travelled a very long way to visit universities and conferences in the metropole, and took care to send papers to their journals. This had its difficulties, but made excellent practical sense. Australian promotion committees are keen on international recognition, but to them 'international' does not mean Mexico or Mozambique. As Harold is aware for climate science, publishing in the North is almost the only way of getting your research noticed globally. In my discipline, the *American Sociological Review* is read all over the world; the Australian and New Zealand *Journal of Sociology* is not. The internet has not changed that.

Elite Northern journals do not need to pay much attention to work published outside the metropole. There is an illuminating article by Robert Tierney and Wei Kan in the *American Educational Research Journal* (*AERJ*) – impact factor 2.157, No. 1 in the league table for education studies. They compared the content of the top education journal in the United States, the *AERJ* itself, with the top education journal in China, *Jiaoyu Yanjiu*. The main style of articles in the two journals was different, and the topics researched also differed, reflecting local policy concerns. But the really striking data were about citations to other scholarship, i.e. the archive in use. Articles in the Chinese journal sometimes referenced US publications. Articles in the US journal *never* referenced Chinese scholarship. Nor did they reference scholarship from other developing countries. Tierney and Kan put it simply: 'the exclusion of Asian and African work from *AERJ* is stark'.[7]

Northern hegemony and Southern extraversion are massive realities that shape the research-based knowledge formation. Hegemony does not mean total domination by the North. Sometimes there are gaps between work in different regions, as Tierney and Kan found between Chinese and US educational research. Sometimes there is a more negotiated connection: many domains of research-based knowledge, from radioastronomy to HIV/AIDS research, *need* a flow of data from the global South. Knowledge workers in the global periphery are far from passive. They develop strategies for participation which include building local research capacities and distinctive research agendas.

The global division of labour did not arise because Europeans were the only people capable of abstract reasoning. It arose because conceptual work in other knowledge formations was excluded, in acts of power.

Making a world university system

Commentators often speak of the globalization of universities as if it were a new trend. Actually it has been happening for nearly five hundred years. The first European-style university in the overseas colonies was a theological college at Santo Domingo, the original Spanish capital in the Caribbean, upgraded to a university by the pope in 1538. It was followed by other colleges in the Spanish empire, and in one British colony a small theological college named after the reverend Mr Harvard. They were followed by a scattering of colleges in colonial seaports around North America and South and East Asia, and eventually many more.

The far-flung universities, from Santo Domingo to Mexico City and Lima, each required a grant of authority by a pope or a king (sometimes both) before they could operate. These charters signalled their official status in the colonies, and affected the vital cultural choice they had to make. Would they reproduce the European curriculum, or would they be open to the indigenous knowledge formations that existed all around them?

This was a real choice. The British East India Company, the band of seafaring robbers who dominated South Asia for a hundred years, founded two colonial colleges in 1781 and 1792. They did not try to clone Oxford and Cambridge. One was called the Calcutta Madrasah, designed to teach Urdu and Islamic jurisprudence, and the other was the Benares Sanskrit College, to teach Sanskrit literature and Hindu law.[8]

But in most colonial colleges and universities, the intention was to teach the culture of the colonizers. The next college set up in British India, the Hindoo College in 1817, was planned to teach English and Bengali. British policy swung hard towards trying to Europeanize the local elites. English language soon predominated, as Spanish already did in the Americas. In the settler colonies of Upper Canada, New South Wales, Victoria, New Zealand and Cape Colony there was no question. Their new universities taught in English, followed English and Scottish curricula, and ignored indigenous knowledge. The University of Sydney, launched in the 1850s, made this crystal clear in the Latin motto it adopted: *sidere mens eadem mutato*: 'under changed skies, the same mind'.

Though this motto suggests a rigid conservatism, back in Europe the universities were already shifting from the text-based curriculum of the classics to the research-based knowledge formation. The historian Tamson Pietsch in her *Empire of Scholars* shows how the settler-colonial universities joined this modernizing trend in the 1870s and 1880s. They shifted towards professional rather than literary education, widened their intake (women undergraduates arrived at this time), and undertook research as the story of Edgeworth David shows.[9]

Through the nineteenth and twentieth centuries the colonial world saw an expanding hierarchy of local colleges, technical and vocational institutes, and universities for indigenous or settler elites. A vocational college was established in Uganda in the 1920s, which became Makerere University, intended as the elite university for British East Africa. In the late nineteenth century Protestant missionaries played the role of an imperial state and began to set up colleges and universities in semi-colonial China, with funds and teachers from the United States.

The Spanish colonies in the Americas won independence early, but conservative, religious forces continued to dominate their universities. The Córdoba student movement sharply rejected that dominance. Their movement was part of a continental wave of university modernization. In 1910 the government in Mexico amalgamated several professional colleges into a nation-building secular university. UNAM, the

National Autonomous University of Mexico, is now one of the great universities of the world – and living proof that modern university architecture can be beautiful. The aristocratic Japanese government, which had fended off colonial rule, had already begun to establish universities as part of its drive for economic development and modernization.

A feature of the colonial and postcolonial university system was a hierarchy of languages. The sociologist Sari Hanafi notes that universities in the Arab east still divide along language lines. Public mass universities teach in Arabic and their staff tend to publish in Arabic for local audiences. Therefore they are, as Hanafi puts it, 'invisible' internationally. Elite private universities, some established by missionaries and some branches of metropolitan universities, are likely to teach in English or French. Local academics who publish internationally – mainly in English or French – are most likely those who have trained in the global North. Even in the 1990s, when there were about 30 universities in sub-Saharan Africa, all taught in English, French, Portuguese or Afrikaans.[10]

By then, English had become the dominant language of research as well as the language of transnational business. The pressure was so great that even institutions specifically designed to preserve other traditions succumbed. Japanese universities, which had kept their native-language model even through an American military occupation, began to give way in the face of the global league tables and the rigid demand for English-language publication in science. The Chinese University of Hong Kong originated in a college set up by refugees from the Communist victory on the mainland. It taught in Chinese language and was intended to preserve Confucian culture. In 2005, however, the university's management shifted policy towards English-language teaching, in the name of internationalization. Despite vehement protests from students and alumni, English is now established. 'Weep for Chinese University', said the characters on a white mourning banner put up in the central square at the time.[11]

In the second half of the twentieth century, many more postcolonial governments followed the Mexican example and established universities as tools of development and symbols of national pride. The need for teachers grew with the vast expansion of elementary and secondary schools. In the atomic age prestige was linked to technology and science. Strategies of economic development through industrialization seemed to require a highly-trained workforce, and UNESCO promoted modernization through education.

In independent India, building on the largest colonial-era university system, the number of universities rose from 30 in 1950–51 to 690 in 2011–12, and the number of colleges increased even more. Most of these were teaching-only, since Indian government policy at first concentrated research in specialized institutes. But with the Jawaharlal Nehru University founded in the 1960s, India too followed the model of an elite central university, with research capability, teaching in English. Regional universities also began to develop postgraduate teaching. At much the same time, the universities in settler-colonial Australia developed substantial research capabilities.[12]

Independent states had the possibility of diverging from colonial models. During the Cold War, the Soviet Union with its polytechnics, research institutes and its ideology of state socialism offered an alternative model to the American research university. This alternative was followed for a time in China, India and the Arab world.

In Africa there was sharp debate whether universities in poor countries should spend their limited resources on research, and whether local cultures and languages should displace those of the colonizers. In 1975 the political scientist Ali Mazrui, who had recently left a senior position at Makerere University, published a powerful critique of academic dependency in African universities. Mazrui argued for 'domesticating' the curriculum; his idea was not to withdraw from global circuits, but to meet local needs, connect with other civilizations besides the European, and expand African and Islamic influence abroad. A decade later, the Kenyan novelist Ngũgĩ wa Thiong'o published his famous essay *Decolonizing the Mind*. In this and later pieces, he rejected neocolonial racism and the exclusion of African thought from academic disciplines, and argued for using local languages. Wa Thiong'o himself began writing and publishing in the Gĩkũyũ language.[13]

But other forces pushed postcolonial universities back into the imperial economy of knowledge. The money and Cold War strategy of the American superpower was one. Together with the Rockefeller, Carnegie and Ford Foundations, the American state invested in universities around the developing world and steered them towards metropolitan models. For instance, the University of Nigeria in the 1960s was partly funded by USAID, and academic staff were seconded there from Michigan State University, joining academics appointed from Britain. France and Britain, as well as the United States, brought bright young men (and a few women) from the periphery for advanced training, and sent them back to be academic leaders – among them, Paulin Hountondji. The geography of the research-based knowledge formation itself pushed in this direction. If a young researcher wanted to do advanced work, whether in biochemistry, plasma physics or economic theory, the most likely place to find good laboratories and research-active colleagues was in the metropole.[14]

What made this turn decisive was the arrival of the neoliberal market agenda in the 1970s and 1980s. In the global South, this meant a turn from balanced, locally driven development, to a search for export advantage in deregulated international markets. Universities in this environment began acting more like corporations, and an increasing number *were* corporations. For-profit private universities have expanded remarkably in South America and South Asia.

An early commercial move was the creation of offshore medical colleges in Caribbean countries, from the 1970s, to take fee-paying students from the United States and Canada. Currently there are about 30 of these colleges.

Their comparative advantages were looser regulation, easier entrance, lower fees and – according to critics – lower standards. There are bigger flows from the periphery towards the metropole. By 2016 there were about 5 million 'international students' in higher education. With steeply rising fees and declining government support, international students have become financial life-blood for the British and Australian university systems, and for particular universities from the United States that are focussed on this market.[15]

It has occurred to many entrepreneurial managers to save fee-paying students the trouble of travelling, and take the universities to them. Not surprisingly they go where the profits are thickest, such as the oil-rich Gulf states. The managers of New York University, an established private university, set up a branch in Abu Dhabi; NYU currently has locations in 12 countries outside the United States. According to the list in Wikipedia, 69 private colleges and university branches, mostly offshore operations, are now found in Dubai. Six US universities and two European universities have branches in the Qatar 'Education City'. These offer courses for local students, for employees of transnational corporations in the region's free-trade zones, and for students from the homeland doing a semester abroad. Their websites are works of art.[16]

Neoliberal ideology celebrates the free market, rolling back the state; but actual states are deeply involved. NYU's expansion depends on support from the US government and on free-trade deals that undermine local public universities. The government of Qatar set up its Education City on the western edge of the capital Doha as a kind of educational free-trade zone. Singapore, whose authoritarian regime has tried to make the island-state a global corporate hub, has also tried to make it a 'Global Schoolhouse'. The effort has been costly, and ran into fiasco in 2007 when the University of New South Wales opened for business there, and closed again after just three months.

The dream of profit still energizes managers and policy-makers, and explains why global ranking systems still carry so much clout. Considered as research, the Shanghai, Times, and QS rankings are embarrassingly bad – muddled in concept, quick-and-dirty in execution, and able to cover only a minority of the world's universities. They were *designed* to highlight the elite Anglo-American research universities. Those favoured by the league tables proceeded to sabotage attempts to construct more sophisticated measures of quality, such as the 'U-Multirank' devised by the European Union.[17]

All ranking systems assume that they are comparing like with like, that all universities are doing the same kind of job in the same kind of environment. That may be true of football teams but it is emphatically not true of education. Nevertheless the rankings have a powerful ideological effect. They construct a fantasy of a homogenized, corporatized world in which each university is a separate firm, competing against all the others. Serving distinctive local needs counts for nothing in the rankings.

Globalization in higher education is partly an illusion, partly a cultural hangover from the old empires, and partly an economic strategy. It already has serious costs. The worldwide expansion of higher education should produce wonderful cultural encounters. That was apparent two centuries ago, even to the East India Company. Qi Xiaoying, who discusses the Qatar and Singapore cases among others, observes that the effect of globalized higher education in its current form has been to concentrate academic power in the metropole and to marginalize local knowledges. The undermining of cultural encounters, she writes sadly, is 'a disappointment of the promise inherent in the notion of education itself'.[18]

Making a worldwide workforce

Disciplines such as physics, linguistics or sociology do not exist as eternal ideas in the mind of God. They appear as institutional practices at particular times and places, and there is very interesting historical research about how this happens.[19]

Sociology, to take the discipline I know best, was brought into existence as an academic formation in the decades around 1900. A bunch of academic entrepreneurs including Albion Small at Chicago, Franklin Giddings in New York and Émile Durkheim in Bordeaux and Paris declared that sociology was a science, no less and no more. They set up teaching and research programmes in universities, formed specialist associations, launched professional journals, and wrote textbooks to codify the science's content. In the opening pages of these textbooks, the reader usually found a passage describing the recent emergence of sociology as a science and naming a pioneering group of twenty or thirty important thinkers in the new field. Almost without exception, they were white, middle-class men residing in the cities of the United States and Europe. Many of them knew each other, wrote to each other and debated with each other.[20]

Something like that happened in most disciplines of the research-based knowledge formation. An elite academic workforce would be defined within the global metropole. Journals and associations would be founded, conferences called, departments set up and textbooks written. The strategy continues today, as new disciplines are constructed (radio-astronomy, molecular biology, computer science, gender studies) or proposed (xenobiology, evolutionary psychology, earth systems science).

Here is how Terry, an Australian professor of chemistry, described the elite network in his field:

> Well, there's quite a close knit – there's no formal structure, but quite a close knit association between, particularly [departments] in the UK and United States and Canada and New Zealand for that matter. But also to a lesser extent but still nevertheless quite useful, with quite a few of the European countries like France and

> Germany in particular, and Holland. There's a like a network, exchange of information about all aspects of [field of chemistry] education. And of course a lot of these people linked each other international conferences which is clearly an important part of it.[21]

We were doing an interview for a study of academic labour and globalization, but it seemed to me that what Terry described was at best a *quasi*-globalization. The invisible colleges at the centre of most disciplines are based in the global metropole, allowing a few researchers from the periphery to join. This is not only a matter of the research elite. The global metropole still produces the bulk of researchers and research publications. A group of Mexican researchers recently put the figures together. In 2010, all of Latin America and the Caribbean put together graduated 15 249 doctoral candidates; in the same year the United States graduated 53 639. Latin American researchers accounted for 4 per cent of world scientific publications, by a commonly used measure.[22]

Disciplinary workforces expanded beyond the metropole in two main ways. The collection of data from the colonized world was one. Linnaeus sent out his travelling Apostles, but soon more botanical data came to the metropole from collectors resident in the colonies. Permanent institutions like the Calcutta Botanic Gardens were set up. Botanical knowledge mattered for settlers and empires – consider spices, maize, cotton, sugar, coffee, timber, tea and rubber – and colonies themselves were often called 'Plantations'.[23] The oil and mining industries, pharmaceutical companies and agribusiness maintain global research workforces today.

The other pathway was the growth of colonial higher education. Collecting and teaching about the local minerals, birds or marriage customs, in the framework of a metropolitan discipline, became normal business for colonial academics like Edgeworth David. On occasion this work attracted the metropole's attention. One could hardly study hominid evolution, for instance, without fossils from Africa. The 1924 discovery of *Australopithecus* in a lime quarry in South Africa became almost as famous as the 1922 discovery of Tutankhamun's tomb in Egypt, and far more important for science. The report on this 'missing link' specimen by Raymond Dart, the young anatomist at the University of Witwatersrand who first studied it, now counts as one of the classic papers in *Nature*.[24]

Initially the workforces in the periphery were small. As late as 1940 the University of Sydney had only 401 full-time staff across all faculties, comprising 222 operations staff and 179 academics. After the mid-century this changed. Australian academic staff – all in public universities at the time – doubled from 1950 to 1960 and grew eight times over by 1980. I have already mentioned the tremendous growth of the Indian university system after independence. Public sector investment drove a very large expansion of the workforce in universities, technical colleges and institutes around the postcolonial world.

In the second half of the twentieth century, we can say, a worldwide intellectual labour force came into existence, based largely, though never wholly, in universities. Its total size was much larger than the metropolitan workforce which had created the system of disciplines in the late nineteenth century. The expanded workforce is now teaching, producing, and circulating disciplinary knowledge on a planetary scale.

This workforce is highly unequal in its incomes, conditions, and resources. There are stark differences between salaries in top universities in the United States and in the regional universities of Africa, South Asia and China. When the Chinese government launched their project to build a group of elite universities, salaries in the happy few doubled; but the project did nothing for rank-and-file universities in China, who protested. Thandika Mkandawire's observations on the thinness of research funding and government support in sub-Saharan Africa have been mentioned already. The feminist scholar Jane Bennett notes that much research on that continent is done in conditions where 'relative chaos, gross economic disparities, displacement, uncertainty and surprise' are the *norm* not the exception. That is true far beyond Africa.[25]

World inequalities create the nagging problem that used to be called the brain drain. The influential anthropologist of science Hebe Vessuri estimated that between 1961 and 1983, some 700 000 professionals emigrated from Latin America to the global North, at an economic cost to the region of something like 30 billion dollars. She called this the 'flight of competencies', and it is very familiar to universities. There are regional flights of competencies too, such as academic migration into South Africa from other parts of sub-Saharan Africa. They create serious difficulties for locally-based knowledge agendas and the building of local workforces.[26]

How is the international workforce connected? Academics connect through the publication system, by email and social media (using that term to cover specialized websites such as *academia.com*), and for those who have access to funds, by travel. Organizations like the International AIDS Society, which has members from 180 countries, or the International Sociological Association, which publishes its magazine *Global Dialogue* in 16 languages, allow links across many countries. Most research projects are local, but a growing number involve multi-country teams. There is a certain traffic in visiting teachers, such as the Michigan State folk who went to the University of Nigeria. Permanent academic migration is a competency drain, but also creates a linking workforce when expatriates keep connected with their home countries.[27]

A complicated skein of connections may therefore exist for any one person. Consider Andre, a biomedical researcher in Brazil whom we interviewed recently. Andre did his degrees locally, and then connected with a WHO project led by famous British and US researchers and funded from the United States. He began travelling – 'Whenever I had a chance to go to the United States I always went there.' In due course he went also to Germany, Scandinavia, Canada and the Netherlands, while keeping research and action projects going in Brazil.[28]

But we must recognize that story as exceptional. For casualized teachers, a growing part of the academic workforce, that kind of 'chance' does not arise. Operations staff also have fewer international connections. Expanding university systems drew from local labour pools for most of their manual, clerical, trades and technical workers. They invested few resources in connecting them with the wider world. I have made a little calculation, and on current wage levels, a janitor at an Indian university who wanted to go to a conference in New York would find that the return economy air fare would wipe out half their *annual* income, and the hotel bills and conference fees would wipe out the other half.

There are, however, connections at the professional and management level. University research administrators, for instance, can be members of professional organizations that are linked in the International Network of Research Management Societies, INORMS, which holds a biennial conference. Vice-chancellors, presidents, provosts and deans of elite universities are funded to travel to conferences and consultations and do so regularly.

The need for participation despite the hierarchies and exclusions is dramatically shown in a recent study of publishing in English. Theresa Lillis and Mary Jane Curry interviewed scholars in Hungary, Slovakia, Spain and Portugal and developed fine-grained text histories of their individual articles. The dominance of English in the global economy of knowledge, and the importance of publishing in top-ranked journals, has created an industry of English-language literacy brokers who help with idiom, style and placement. They are paid by researchers from the periphery or semi-periphery who hope to break into the charmed circle. This is far from being a world of free and equal flows. Lillis and Curry put it simply: 'global' is a place called the 'US'.[29]

Multiple knowledge formations and Southern theory

Are these global hierarchies inevitable?

When the first waves of data-collectors came out from the imperial centre, they relied on guides, translators and informants from indigenous peoples, who told them about land and sea, plants and animals, cultures and societies. In short, the collectors tapped local knowledge. Some acknowledged the appropriation, many did not; it mattered little after the data got to the metropole. But while the imperial knowledge economy grew, the local knowledge refused to die.

This is powerfully shown by Margaret Somerville and Tony Perkins' *Singing the Coast*, telling the stories of a displaced Aboriginal community in north-eastern New South Wales: there is resilience even under the genocidal pressures of settler colonialism. In other parts of the colonized world formal knowledge institutions continued, such as the schools of Islamic knowledge called *madrassa*, though their social and political meaning changed. There are recognized knowledge-holders, such as the elders and storytellers of indigenous communities, the practitioners of Ayurvedic medicine in South Asia, and the scholarly *ulama* of the Islamic world. Perhaps the most striking example of continuity is the great centre of scholarship in Sunni Islam, the al-Azhar university in Egypt, which I discuss in Chapter 7.[30]

Ali Mazrui's critique of academic dependency in Africa relied on these facts. He knew of alternatives to imperial science, including whole civilizations with origins independent of Europe, and their well-developed knowledge formations. These include the locally-based indigenous knowledge systems emphasized by decolonial theory. They also include alternative universalisms, such as Islamic knowledge, or the Gandhian perspectives developed by scholars such as Vinay Lal.[31]

The imperial economy of knowledge, then, has never lived alone. Boaventura de Sousa Santos puts it well: there is an ecology of knowledges. So when university staff and students take up the issue of decolonizing the curriculum, from the 'Nairobi Literature Debate' of 1968–74 to the current 'Why Is My Curriculum White?' campaign in Britain, they have alternatives to point to.

Those urging alternatives often argue as if different knowledge formations were inherently and sharply distinct. Ngũgĩ wa Thiong'o drew a clear line, amounting to a political opposition, between literature or orature in local languages, and literature in the languages of the colonizers such as English and French. Santos speaks of 'abyssal' gaps between colonizer and colonized, and Kathy Luckett speaks of a 'collective hermeneutic gap' in contemporary South Africa. We can recognize the violence of colonization without accepting such divisions as fundamental to knowledge. Bibi Bakare-Yusuf, in her critique of a well-known Afrocentric text on gender, argued that African cultures before colonization were not sharply separate from each other. They interacted, evolved, and registered distant influences. Ngũgĩ wa Thiong'o himself argued:

> Local knowledge is not an island unto itself: it is part of the main, part of the sea. Its limits lie in the boundless universality of our creative potentiality as human beings.

The creative interplay of knowledge formations seems an important and well-established historical fact.[32]

As well as recognizing indigenous knowledge formations and alternative universalisms, we need to pay attention to knowledge generated from the colonial encounter, and from colonial and postcolonial social dynamics. This is what I have called 'Southern theory'. Given the long history of colonialism and neocolonial forms of global power, it is a large field. Let me list a few classics:

- Huamán Poma's astonishing *Nueva corónica* of about 1615, telling the history of Inca empire and Spanish conquest, and documenting the brutality of colonial society;

- Kartini's critique of the subordination of women in colonial Java, and He-Yin Zhen's critique of the subordination of women in semi-colonial China, both around the turn of the twentieth century;
- Frantz Fanon's analysis of the psychological consequences of racism and colonial power, and Raúl Prebisch and Samir Amin's economics of global inequality, in the mid-twentieth century;
- Bina Agarwal's *A Field of One's Own* on gender and land in postcolonial South Asia, and Achille Mbembe's *Critique of Black Reason* on the coloniality of philosophy, near the turn of the twenty-first century.

The intellectuals of colonial and postcolonial societies certainly produce theory, and have done so throughout that history.

So far, most theory produced in the global South has had little influence in the dominant economy of knowledge. Fanon and Freire are exceptional in being well known in the North. But the research-based knowledge formation is not static, and some fields are responding to critique. Gender studies is one. Fairly recently institutionalized, it has generated its own critiques of Eurocentrism, and has developed South/South connections. Some Northern journals have made efforts to highlight global-South feminist research.[33]

There is increasing documentation, too, of how research techniques can be tied to Southern needs and experience. An example is the work of Cheikh Mbow, a climate researcher in Senegal. Trained in a French research system, Mbow started with the familiar paradigm of Northern theory and Southern data. But he worked through to an autonomous stance, where he was able to challenge his mentors – both modifying their methods for local realities, and developing an interest in local communities' knowledge.[34]

Challenges are also made to the institutional machinery of global hierarchy, such as the under-representation of

Latin America in Northern-based bibliographical databases. An unusually high proportion of Latin American research journals are now published with Open Access, accessible to anyone online. The region created its own bibliographical databases covering local journals, most famously SciELO (Scientific Electronic Library Online). To get wider circulation, Brazilian policy prescribes that a percentage of papers in local journals should be published in English. In the same spirit CLAM, the excellent Latin American Centre in Sexuality and Human Rights at the State University of Rio de Janeiro, made a collection of the region's sexuality and gender research available in English, online. It is not yet clear how much of a dent these efforts have made in global hierarchy. What is clear is that Latin American scholarship is now as freely available as scholarship anywhere on earth. And that is something to cheer for.[35]

The global workforce, then, has more room for manoeuvre than the bald facts of Northern hegemony and Southern extraversion might suggest. Researchers and teachers can respond to regional needs, develop distinctive research centres and agendas, renovate curricula and create links with local communities, while staying within the research-based knowledge formation. It is also possible, though more difficult, for university staff to move outside the dominant knowledge formation, connect with other formations and move towards epistemological pluralism.

We should never regard the economy of knowledge as monolithic or immutable. It will certainly change. In what direction, will be decided by struggles in which knowledge workers themselves, especially in the global South, will be central.

Chapter 5

Privilege machines

The dark side of the university

The eight universities where I have taught have all been places of privilege. Money is proclaimed by glittering buildings, costly computers, tidy lawns, and the well-cut business suits of rectors, presidents and vice-chancellors. At inner-city universities, there is often a shocking contrast between the wealth on campus and the poverty across the street.

There is a great deal of evidence about privilege and universities. Here is a sample. National data from 1973 in Scotland revealed that the children of white-collar workers had six times the rate of entry to university that the children of manual workers had. National data from Australia in the mid-1990s, a time of expansion in the university system, showed that 'Both commencing and total enrolments are strongly biased towards high socio-economic status students'. National data from South Africa in 2013 showed a university participation rate for White youth of 55 per cent, for Black youth 16 per cent. A national sample survey in Egypt, in the same year, found that students coming from the wealthiest 20 per cent of families make up 55 per cent of youth in public universities and 65 per cent in private universities. But the effect starts much earlier: according to national data, students from the selective academic high schools in Egypt have a transition rate to higher education of 80.7 per cent while students from vocational high schools, the majority, have a transition rate of 8.9 per cent. Recent data from Poland, at a time when the university system had stopped expanding, show that a person whose parents had a university education has more than ten times the chance of going to university than people whose parents did not.[1]

One suspects something systematic is going on.

Consider one case more closely: rural–urban inequalities in post-Soviet Georgia, the subject of a careful study by Maia Chankseliani. In 2005 the Georgian government introduced standardized tests, the Unified National Examinations (UNE), to overcome corruption in access to higher education. Urban students generally do better on these tests than rural students do. Some reasons are shown in Chankseliani's interviews with rural students' families. They include absolute poverty in the villages and families, unfamiliarity with the higher education system, and poorly resourced schools (many educational services in the countryside collapsed when the communist regime fell). When all other things are statistically equal, rural students who do the UNE tests have a higher admission rate than urban students. But rural students mostly apply to lower-prestige, regional universities, which are cheaper and more accessible. And farther in the background is more filtering, on a huge scale. Only a quarter of rural high school students in Georgia ever sit for the UNE, compared with half of the urban students. And a lower percentage of rural youth go to high school in the first place. A whole ecology of advantage and disadvantage produces large differences in the final outcomes.[2]

The dramatic global expansion of higher education in the last generation has not eliminated large inequalities in access. Simon Marginson sadly observes: 'Stratification effects trump the equalization of educational quantity through growth'. Mignonne Breier puts it more bluntly: poverty matters.[3]

Why the inequalities in access? Material reasons are in front of our noses. Most universities charge fees, and the fees plus other costs are beyond what most poor people can pay. Marginson quotes figures from the United States where average college tuition fees in 2011 represented 9 per cent of annual income for the top 20 per cent of families, but 114 per cent of annual income for the bottom 20 per cent – and that was before paying for food and housing. In Breier's data, sheer lack of money was the commonest reason for dropout from South African universities, even after students managed to get there; and in South Africa, mass poverty is Black. Most universities are in cities, especially elite universities: not accessible for peasant and pastoral communities. Most universities have admission requirements that require years of full-time study in secondary school, preferably in an academic not a vocational programme; most poor kids do not stay so long in school. Richer parents can pay for better tutoring when students prepare for entrance examinations. Universities often draw students from feeder secondary schools that are themselves socially privileged, especially expensive private schools.

If wealth and poverty seem too crude an explanation, some sociologists have emphasized cultural differences. Basil Bernstein found technical differences in the language of English working-class and middle-class families, and built a highly influential theory of mismatch between the language practices of formal schooling and those of working-class students. Pierre Bourdieu emphasized showy differences of cultural style that the gatekeepers of elite French institutions looked for in examinations. Bourdieu called this kind of difference 'cultural capital' and it became the centrepiece of his theorizing of social reproduction through education.

The problem with reproduction theories is that they are basically theories of difference, providing an automatic mechanism that stabilizes a system of inequality. This is the role of Bourdieu's enormously influential concept of 'habitus', the internalized tendency to produce a defined pattern of behaviour, whether a style of writing or a way of holding the body. The difficulty is that the effect of social reproduction is built into the definition of habitus, assuming a self-contained social system. European social structure has not been self-contained for centuries and does not reliably reproduce itself, while colonized societies have been violently disrupted. We cannot presume an automatic process here; cultural differences are actively produced and are sites of struggle, where privileged groups may win or may lose.[4]

Other sociologists have emphasized the active defence of social boundaries, 'social closure'. Frank Parkin defined this as 'collective social action designed to maximize claims to rewards and opportunities'. In plain English, that means an attempt to grab scarce resources by fending off competing claimants. The deliberate exclusion of women from universities makes sense when seen as defence of the privileges of men. Racial exclusions work the same way, in defence (mainly) of White privilege. The recent explosion in credentials makes good sense when they are seen as attempts at social closure in a changing economy. The approach also gives some grip on why a minority of elite universities has not only survived but flourished, despite the apparent democratization of education. The concept of closure, however, leaves mysteries about how particular groups get the capacity to close resources off, and how education can operate as a privilege.[5]

Here, approaches from political economy have more traction. Marginson, for instance, treats higher education as a 'positional good'. He is healthily sceptical of the idea that education itself produces economic returns. What counts is the struggle of middle-class families for *relative* advantage in competitive and insecure labour markets. On this view, the hierarchy of universities and colleges is not a historical accident. Differences in prestige and in access to networks are essential to the system. Worse, there is a historical ratcheting-up at work.

Expansion of the higher education system increases the pressure of competition, and the pressure for further expansion of credentials and numbers. But the shift towards funding this expansion by student fees – even China introduced fees in 1997 – creates road-blocks for the poor.

Out of political economy came an even bolder approach to universities. Sheila Slaughter and Larry Leslie, studying universities in Anglophone countries, proposed the concept of 'academic capitalism' to describe the growing attempts to make money in the market by selling services – particularly consultancies and research – and competing for fee-paying students. Recent work by the German sociologist Richard Münch ties the concept of academic capitalism more closely to the research-based knowledge formation. In his analysis, what was formerly a knowledge commons, held in trust by the academic community as a whole, is increasingly privatized as corporate-style managers gain control of universities. A cycle develops where the enterprise-university invests its money to gain prestige, and cashes in the prestige – via student fees, research grants, etc. – to gain more funds.[6]

Clearly there is some truth in these ideas, and I will explore them further in the next chapter. Managerial universities do act like corporations, trying to extract rent from their discoveries and selling access to their courses. Exclusions protect the value of these assets, so the academic-capitalism thesis gives some grip on why the contemporary university system involves so much inequality. But there are also problems here. The most ruthless of privatizers runs up against the research-based knowledge formation itself, with its need to circulate knowledge and its habits of cooperation. There are popular demands for access to knowledge that are not easily contained within market policies: even poor people may feel they have a right to education!

Further, the academic-capitalism thesis underplays the power of the state in designing, funding, and re-shaping university systems. The state may speak loudly about access.

Who needs subtle theory when confronted with the 'Cooks Circular' issued by the Russian imperial authorities in 1887? This splendid document forbade the academic high schools, which gave access to universities, to enrol:

> children of coachmen, menials, cooks, washerwomen, small shopkeepers, and the like. For, excepting occasionally gifted children, it is completely unwarranted for the children of such people to leave their position in life.[7]

The same regime imposed quotas on Jews in higher education, and tried to prevent teaching in local languages. Yet by the outbreak of the Great War in 1914, Russian state investment had produced the largest higher education system in Europe. It had a strong representation of women, and many working-class students on scholarships – including, one suspects, the children of cooks.

These explanations of inequality are not stark alternatives. They focus on different mechanisms, which can interact. In Georgia, for instance, state strategy introduced centralized examinations for university entry, but then cultural and economic differences along class and regional lines affected how those examinations worked. The dramatic 1987–89 shift in university policy in Australia, when a Labor Party government introduced market mechanisms, was in part an attempt to widen access. But the tools used, including tuition fees and sharper competition, rapidly produced new inequalities in which – surprise! – the old ruling-class universities, colloquially known as 'the sandstones', came out on top. In 2007 Kang Xiaoguang made a pithy critique of links between the government and the urban rich in China:

> It is an alliance whereby the elites collude to pillage the masses.

Not only in China.[8]

Making advantage happen

The weakness of many discussions of unequal access is that they treat universities and schools as passive: places where pre-existing cultural differences, or family wealth, or class power, become manifest. These structures and forces are certainly at work. But it is vital to recognize that universities and schools themselves are highly active in *making* inequalities.[9]

This could be seen right from the start of the colonial expansion, with new universities closely tied to the colonizing power. Almost all of them excluded local knowledge formations in favour of the text-based curriculum from the metropole. By that stroke, the prior knowledge of most of the world's population was made useless for access to university education.

As the closure model emphasizes, universities give credentials, and that means excluding the uncredentialled, as well as legitimating the skills of the credentialled. The history of professions such as medicine revolves around the exclusion of unqualified practitioners – a key means of discrediting women healers such as midwives.

In the 1970s a discussion began about 'credentials inflation'. This meant both the multiplication of new qualifications, and the demand for higher credentials where lower ones used to be enough. Universities have been active on both fronts. They have taken over training for professions such as accountancy, teaching and nursing, and increased the required length of study, for instance replacing a one-year Diploma of Education with a two-year Master of Teaching. They have shifted lucrative courses such as medicine from undergraduate to graduate programmes. Most impressively, they have created new qualifications in fields such as strategic communication (advertising), urban land economics (real estate), and of course business management.[10]

The expansion of higher education has tended to stratify workforces regardless of the field of knowledge. Being university-trained *in itself* became a kind of credential and a source of privilege. This has been controversial in parts of the global South where graduate *un*employment grew in the late twentieth century, when national development programmes stalled. Investing in technical schools was proposed, meeting social needs better. But uncertainty in a market context increases the pressure for the most prestigious form of credentials, to get a generic advantage. So the growth of universities continued, regardless of the relevance or quality of what they were offering.

Like elite schools, universities create solidarity among the privileged. The male-only colleges of Oxford and Cambridge, the men's clubs of the old German universities, the Greek-letter fraternities of North America, created relationships of friendship, patronage, shared identity, and sometimes sexual partnership, that lasted into later life. University managers' pursuit of endowments and grants from wealthy alumni give them a major interest in fostering social networks centred on universities. The US cult of college football has more to do with networks than with healthy recreation in the fresh air. R. D. Anderson's splendid history of European higher education in the nineteenth century traces universities' role in creating professional and bureaucratic elites in the metropole – as they were intended to. This effort has continued in new conditions, as social structures and global relationships have changed.[11]

The role of business schools is particularly significant. At first modelled on training programmes for state officials, in the early twentieth century business schools in the United States – at Pennsylvania, Dartmouth, Harvard and Chicago – became linked with the national corporate elite. But as corporate businesses became more global in their operations, the elite business schools began carefully to internationalize their intake of students. The MBA is now a well-recognized way to prepare for a managerial career in the global corporate economy. It is being offered in much the same form in universities around the world, in poor countries as well as rich. The MBA is *not* a professional qualification in the ordinary sense of a research-based training for specialized service to clients. More important than that, it is a pathway to power, deliberately non-specialized.[12]

In one of the great ironies of university history, something similar happened under communism. The original plan was to educate a new socialist intelligentsia. In China, the People's Republic took over the relatively new Renmin University, re-named it the People's University of China, and made it a cadre college to educate Party activists. In Bulgaria, like other Soviet-backed regimes, the new government proposed to purge bourgeois students in favour of the children of workers and peasants. Without much delay, these mechanisms of transformation became mechanisms of corruption. Supporters of the regime got privileged access to higher education, and – as the Hungarian dissidents Konrád and Szelényi put it – via the party and the state, intellectuals were on the road to class power. The party-states of eastern Europe crumbled after 1989, but all was not lost. Their cadres re-invented themselves as professional and business elites, and passed their privilege on to the next generation. Renmin University too has put its revolutionary past into cold storage. It is now part of the Chinese elite university system, carefully following US models and deeply committed to competition.[13]

These stories give some plausibility to the idea that universities today are constructing a global corporate elite, or a global middle class. Among the signs are the international spread of the MBA; the merging of both public and private sector management with computer technology; the rise of English as the language of international business, science and elite university education; and the international migration of students. Perhaps Konrád and Szelényi's idea was just premature? I think an integrated global elite is a possible future, but not an accomplished fact. Chunks of global power are held by dictatorships, economic oligarchs, transnational managers, and military and state elites – overwhelmingly men, it should be noted. There is privilege in the background, but is hard to see this array as unified through higher education.

Much clearer is the role of today's universities in *legitimating* inequalities. No university president opens their mouth in public without the word 'excellence' floating out. The lightning-fast embrace of shonky league tables is a sign of the ideological work being done. Managers' usual reaction to each year's rankings is not to question the system, but to boast when they can, and try to lever their own university a notch higher. Except at Harvard, which is already sitting in the top notch, and which pretends to appoint only the most excellent academics in the world.

Recently, wherever I walked on the University of Sydney campus I was confronted with banners extolling 'leadership'. The same slogan was used off-campus in the university's advertising. Staff and students were not invited to discuss what this concept actually meant, or why our managers were now promoting the fascist *Führerprinzip*. It was just presented to the public as the meaning of the university. That was a particularly tasteless example, but far from isolated. A great deal of university publicity presents competitive success as what is most valued.

The university system itself models hierarchy. Europe has a set of prestigious universities with long-established ruling-class connections. Across the Atlantic, a similar position is held by the Ivy League universities such as Columbia and Yale, and elite private universities modelled on them such as Chicago and Stanford. These can usefully be thought of as the group of aristocratic universities. They once serviced the churches and the landed gentry, and in due course the new business elites; they sneered at public universities in industrial cities (in Britain called 'redbrick' after the handsome 1892 Victoria Building at the upstart University of Liverpool) and the land-grant colleges of the United States.

It was only with pain that the aristocratic universities weathered the transition to the research-based knowledge formation, wistfully looking back to the 'Great Books of the Western World' (Hutchins, at Chicago), the 'Great Tradition' (Leavis, at Cambridge), or the 'Western Canon' (Bloom, at Yale). But survive it they did, and their prestige has been maintained by academic selection, high fees, and endowment by new corporate wealth.[14]

In the neoliberal era, integrated public systems have been deliberately broken up. Policy shifts and management strategies have widened gaps between universities. The 'U15' group in Canada (1991), the 'Russell Group' in the UK (1994), and the 'Group of 8' in Australia (1999) are self-appointed minorities claiming elite status and lobbying for their own benefit – 'leading excellence', according to the Go8's semi-literate website. I have mentioned the Chinese state's funding of a small group of 'world-class universities', a vague rhetorical term that has become remarkably popular. The rot has even reached Germany, which has a stronger commitment to public higher education than almost any other country. The German government's 'excellence initiative' of 2005–17 targeted 'universities of excellence' for special funding – and found they were not easy to define.[15]

The rhetoric is so loud that it is easy to miss the consequence. This language defines the great majority of universities as *not* excellent, *not* world-class. Real legitimacy lives only in the narrow circle of the most privileged, the One Per Cent of the university world. Once upon a time, bishops and kings provided their societies with an ideology of hierarchy. Now, the university system does.

Breaching the walls

In 1995 Australia's national Higher Education Council came to review questions of fairness. It studied the situation of six 'equity groups': women, indigenous people, migrants of non-English-speaking background, people with disabilities, rural people, and 'people from socio-economically disadvantaged backgrounds'. In India, where measures to overcome social exclusion include reservation of places in public universities, the officially recognized disadvantaged groups are the Scheduled Castes, Scheduled Tribes, Other Backward Classes, and the Muslim minority. Together these add up to nearly 80 per cent of the population.[16]

This looks like serious recognition for problems of equity. But what does it mean in practice? In Indian universities, 70 years after independence, the Hindu upper castes still have startlingly higher enrolment ratios than any other groups. When the Australian Higher Education Council got down to tin tacks, it noted that government funding for the national equity programme amounted to five million dollars a year, in a higher education budget of five *thousand* million. The Council hoped that universities were kicking in extra money from their other funds; but no national initiative followed. The Higher Education Council, however, has been abolished.

One reform movement has had massive success, and this is worth attention. A few women gained degrees from European universities in the enlightenment era. They were obliged to study privately: the regular lectures were only for men. Elena Lucrezia Cornaro Piscopia, a Venetian philosopher, is said to have been the first woman awarded the PhD (in the cathedral at Padova in 1678). This remained highly unusual until the nineteenth century, when a wider feminist movement emerged. The aristocratic universities resisted reform. Male professors and doctors cooked up an astonishing stew of ideas about women's weaker brains: intellectual effort was seen as a health risk, threatening women's God-given duty of having lots of children.[17]

Ignoring these fantasies, bourgeois women moved into the university world. They followed two strategies: building separate colleges for women, and agitating for entry to men's institutions. Women began attending lectures at the University of London practically from its start, in the 1830s. By the time of the Great War, women were a substantial minority of university students across the global metropole and in settler-colonial countries. They were concentrated in programmes like teacher education, and gender segregation was maintained in everyday life with separate residences, separate clubs and so on; but women's collective presence was established.[18]

The consequences matured in the later twentieth century with the Women's Liberation movement and equal-rights policies. Education is a specific target in the 1979 UN Convention on the Elimination of all forms of Discrimination Against Women (CEDAW). In many countries women are now a majority of the students in higher education, a mass presence. Women's numbers have been increasing in academic roles and in university administration, though we do not yet have parity in senior roles. The radical wing of Women's Liberation went on to challenge the knowledge formation itself, seeing the whole university curriculum as a patriarchal construction. Within a decade a new domain of knowledge had crystallized, first known as Women's Studies and then Gender Studies, with an apparatus of research journals, associations, conferences and named degrees.[19]

These gains have required unending struggle against resistance by powerful men and the hidden curriculum of male entitlement. Men still dominate in physical sciences, business, engineering and biomedical research. In 2007 the journal *Feminist Africa* surveyed the scene across that continent, and found continuing activism by women on issues like sexual harassment, but limited reform of institutions. Managers rarely gave firm commitment to Women's Studies, male-dominated student cultures were conservative, and curriculum change was slow. In 2016 the Human Rights Commission in Australia ran a large survey of students in all the country's universities. Almost one woman in three reported having been sexually harassed in a university setting *during that year*. Universities have mostly ended gender exclusion, but are still sites of backlash, complacency, entitlement and inertia.[20]

Access for working-class and peasant students has been even more of a struggle. Mass elementary schooling, imagined during the Reformation by the great Czech educator Jan Amos Komensky (Comenius), became a reality in the nineteenth-century metropole and colonies of settlement. Labour movements demanded that further education too should be opened to working-class children. State patronage made this possible for a minority, and the 'scholarship boy' became a recognized figure at a time when universities were still usually seen as bastions of class privilege.

Working-class parties eventually came to see universities as part of the welfare state or the new socialist society, and supported the mid-twentieth-century expansion. In that remote era, capitalists too supported public investment in education! Part-time study and distance education opened degree courses to a wider public. Though it was mainly white-collar workers who benefited, some children of manual workers also arrived as 'first in family' students. The Soviet regime went harder for technical higher education, to support rapid industrialization. Later left-wing regimes have also tried to expand and democratize higher education. In the twenty-first century, Venezuela and Brazil established new public universities, took higher education to remote regions, and tried to increase participation from Black and indigenous communities. In South Africa, the struggle against apartheid was waged in universities as well as schools, attempting to widen access and develop emancipatory methods.[21]

However important locally, these initiatives have been dwarfed by the worldwide effects of the market turn. For-profit private colleges specialize in vocational courses, and many offer direct contact with potential employers. They respond to the growing insecurity of labour markets, as well as to state under-investment in education. For these reasons they have had quick and impressive success, enrolling a growing proportion of working-class students in Brazil and India as well as the United States. Transnational corporations soon got into the act. In 2012 Claudio Rama published a study of their move into Latin American higher education. He found an impressive array, including Laureate, Withney, Apollo (owner of Phoenix) and Education Management Corporation (part-owned by Goldman Sachs) from the United States, Pearson from the UK, as well as big Brazilian firms.[22]

The expansion of private universities and colleges is a money-making operation, not a social justice reform. It has not dented even slightly the hierarchy of universities. Most of the working-class organizations that pressed for educational access – socialist parties and labour unions – have been disastrously weakened in the neoliberal era. It is now difficult to find any university system in the world where policy gives robust priority to higher education for working-class or peasant communities.

Of course market-regime governments say they are committed to equity and opportunity. Of course elite universities display their commitment to diversity. They speak of recruiting bright students whose background is 'low SES' (socio-economic status is the current euphemism for class). They offer more scholarships to indigenous students, train 'allies' for gay students and promote 'leadership' for women. Perhaps some angst about social justice is still being felt in the executive suites.

Machine limits

I called this chapter 'Privilege Machines' to emphasize that inequalities are produced by institutions, not just by the prejudices of individual gatekeepers. Fees, selection mechanisms, organizational cultures, curricula and so forth really matter. But we should not forget that institutionalized inequalities shape human lives. One of the most poignant stories is the struggle of Dalit students, from the 'untouchable' castes, to gain an education in India's universities. Susie Tharu describes a ceremony for students from these castes, in which the young people about to go to university are warned to be hardworking, quiet, and thick-skinned, i.e. not to challenge discrimination. Tharu observes that this advice contradicts what universities are supposed to be for. But these students will face a lot of discrimination, and many suicides result:

> In each case the story was one of repeatedly getting bad grades, of being confronted with unmanageable cut-offs and deadlines, impatient and dismissive teachers, supervisors unwilling to take them on ...[23]

One such suicide, by the Dalit student Rohit Vemula, triggered the bitter upheaval about caste oppression and official inaction at the University of Hyderabad in 2016.[24]

It is hard for university staff to accept that our beloved institutions do such things, that our own regular labour has despicable results. Yet we cannot shrug off inequalities by attributing them only to outside causes. We may not intend injustice, but the university collectively produces it, and we have to take our share of responsibility for it.

Responsibility implies that there is some choice, that things could be otherwise. What processes in universities and the economy of knowledge offer alternatives? When we ask this question, there is more reason for hope. There are forces that limit the privilege machines and point towards more democratic universities and university systems.

One is the research-based knowledge formation at the centre of modern university life. It is true that this was designed mainly by White middle-class men, and is hegemonized by the global North. Influential figures and research centres accumulate prestige and funds. (In a traditional joke in the sociology of science, this is called the Matthew Effect, after a sentence in the Gospel of Matthew, 'unto every one that hath shall be given ... but from him that hath not shall be taken away'.)[25]

But the knowledge formation contains a powerful imperative to circulate and share knowledge widely. This is shown specifically by the Open Access movement, and generally by the requirement to publish. Active research fields work on a peer-to-peer basis, with contributions pouring in from new players. Key researchers do appear, but rarely remain at the cutting edge for very long. Einstein, twenty years after his miraculous debut in 1905, was fading from the lead in physics; the same befell Chomsky in linguistics after his astonishing *Syntactic Structures*. The whole knowledge formation moves via critique of the archive. Critical thought is necessary to research-based knowledge, and that can subvert hierarchy as brilliantly as any anarchist plot.

Another countervailing force is the humanist culture of the university workforce. I hesitate to use this term, given fundamentalist polemics against an imaginary 'secular humanism', and post-structuralist polemics against giving too much importance to the human subject. But 'humanist' is a traditional term for something much broader. It stands for the university's role in the general advancement of learning, the study of literary, artistic, religious and scientific treasures, and reflection on God and nature, society, fate and the future. It stands for the educational purposes evoked by the old idea of *Bildung* and the newer one of education for global citizenship.

Humanism in this sense is widespread among university staff. Operations staff often value working for a university because it serves a public purpose along these lines. Most academics in the sciences as well as in Arts faculties have a sense of the broad cultural purposes of the university. This is significant for issues about privilege because the underlying stance in university humanism is inclusive. It gives in-principle support to the spread of education and the sharing of knowledge and culture. We may be sceptical of grand declarations, but it is easy to find support among university staff for equal opportunity measures, programmes for indigenous students, online popular education (for example the multi-university theconversation.com), or international exchanges. I think a widespread humanist culture sustains the resistance in universities to crass commercialization and corporate-style management.[26]

Two major forces from outside universities also limit the privilege machines. Social movements of the oppressed have persistently demanded wider access to higher education, and more attention by universities to social needs. They have had a striking impact. Who would have thought, two hundred years ago, that women might become a majority among university students? Who would have thought, one hundred years ago, there would be mass university systems in former colonies? These things have come about by social pressure and many mobilizations. Episodic as they are, mobilizations around higher education still happen, as the 2011 student revolt in Chile and the 2015 Fees Must Fall movement in South Africa remind us.

Finally, we should not forget the state! Governments have an interest in economic growth, advanced training for their national workforces, and research as a driver of industrial growth and military power. Some political parties come to office with working-class support and democratic agendas for education. Equal opportunity and anti-discrimination laws have impacted universities; new universities have been founded to serve disadvantaged groups or regions; and equity policies circulate through inter-governmental agencies such as UNESCO, UN Women, and bilateral aid programmes.

Universities are not, generally speaking, noted for their democratic ways. Individual departments can be pocket-sized tyrannies; income inequalities within universities are growing; hierarchies of rank and authority are usual. But there are many incoherencies and even contradictions in universities as organizations. There is a tension between the imperative of expansion and the logic of social closure. Research-based knowledge is unpredictable, and university managers face risks whenever they try to direct research through 'strategic initiatives', picking winners and anointing star researchers.

In public university budgets – edited versions can be read online – the two big sources of income are regular operating grants from government tax revenue, and fees from students. They represent conflicting concepts of what a university is for: the public interest, or the private benefit of university-firms and their customers. In the neoliberal era the balance has shifted far towards private benefit. But that opens tensions between university staff and university managers, about the share of revenues that should go to wages. It opens tensions between staff and students over academic standards, fees, 24/7 online availability, and more.

Universities are loosely articulated organizations rather than tight ones. They are also vulnerable. Flows of incoming students are not guaranteed. Student migrations shift from one destination to another, and this possibility can be used, as the Chinese and Saudi governments showed in 2018, to create pressure in international politics. Flows of research funds are not guaranteed. The whole research economy created by Cold War federal programmes in the United States has faded. Universities as working institutions can be disrupted by abrupt cuts in government funding, by strikes and student occupations, or by police and military interventions.

Universities have benefited enormously in the past from public respect for research and higher education. This attitude can no longer be taken for granted. Attacks on research-based knowledge, most recently those funded by fossil fuel magnates against climate science, have gained dangerous levels of support. Meanwhile the rise of market ideology since the 1970s has been undermining all collective, public-interest projects. Universities themselves have become increasingly complicit with market ideology. To understand this tangle we need a closer look at the managerial takeover, the focus of the next chapter.

Chapter 6

The university business

The maelstrom

The face of the modern university, as it smiles out from the television news, is a neat middle-aged man or woman in a well-cut business suit, speaking with confidence about markets, league tables and excellence. There is no shadow of an ivory tower on this face, and rightly so. Universities have long been close to power-holders, whether bishops, bureaucrats or businessmen. They have naturally been swept up in the worldwide transformation of government and economic life in the last 40 years.[1]

The commonest name for this transformation is 'neoliberalism'. The word suggests a coherent and kindly philosophy, rather than the turbulent, coercive and sometimes violent changes that have actually happened. I will use 'neoliberalism' only for the ideological agenda of competition, privatization and individualism. I will call the organizational changes 'managerialism'; and the institutional and policy environment that universities now face, the 'market regime'. The violence I will call violence.[2]

In 2001 Susan Stokes published a book with the sub-title *Neoliberalism by Surprise in Latin America*, and in 2007 Naomi

Klein published a book called *The Shock Doctrine*. The phrases are apt. It is rare for the people in any part of the world to *vote* to sell off public assets, reduce public services, pay higher fees or make incomes more unequal. A market regime is usually installed top-down, by some kind of coup. That includes proper, bloodstained military takeovers, including the 1973 coup in Chile whose violence ushered in the first full-blown market regime in any country. Another kind of coup is the demand for 'structural adjustment', enforced by international debt. That became familiar to Mexico and Argentina in the 1980s, and is still on the books, as Greece discovered in 2012–15. Organizations too have been transformed by surprise. Indeed there have been thousands of perfectly legal coups where a group of entrepreneurs first got control at the top, then launched a managerial agenda, steamrolling opposition as they went.

Neoliberalism is more than a dogmatic version of free-market economics. In the global South it was introduced as a new development strategy, exploiting cheap labour and natural resources for export income. In the global North it meant a shift in the corporate world from long-term planning to maximizing short-term gains. Deregulation opened the way to a great boom in finance and the innovations of 'platform capitalism', the mixture of technology, advertising and surveillance seen in Facebook and Google. The logic of short-term gain was quickly applied to social resources. Previous generations had built many institutions to meet collective needs: cooperatives, professional associations, government departments, hospitals, schools, kindergartens, transport systems, prisons, sports codes, and more. Businessmen found a vast field of opportunity here. If they got control, they could change the way these institutions worked and tap them for streams of profit.

The cascade did not take long to reach universities. As a report on the future of universities by the management consultancy Ernst & Young put it:

> We foresee very large opportunities for the private sector.[3]

Indeed the private sector has not waited. Witness the British-based corporation Informa plc, with more than 7000 employees, which publishes academic journals and will run your academic conference, for a fee. Hanover Research, a US-based operation, will sell you advice on how to brand your university, which is vital because:

> a brand can also provide a sense of values, culture, and vision to current students and employees.[4]

Other corporations have taken the direct route, and have bought or built their own for-profit universities. The biggest is Laureate Education, a US company, which claims to own about 70 universities with a million students; this group paid Bill Clinton more than 16 million dollars to be a figurehead chancellor. The league tables too are constructed by for-profit corporations, which sell the rankings and stories to news media – and then sell advice to universities on how to improve their individual rankings. Close to blackmail? Perish the thought! It is just a business opportunity.[5]

Corporations did not initiate the market regime for universities: market-friendly governments did. University presidents and vice-chancellors hammer this point when they talk about their problems, and they are quite right. Shifts in higher education policy have arrived, in country after country, as part of the installation of a broader market regime. The strategy has been promoted across the world by intergovernmental economic agencies, notably the World Bank and the OECD. María Olivia Mönckeberg, who has made a close study of the surge of private universities in Chile, notes their connection with specific groups holding political power in the neoliberal state. A good deal of the profit in private universities actually comes from government subsidies or government-guaranteed loans for fees.[6]

The cascade began in Chile with the 'New Law of Universities', a package of measures by the Pinochet dictatorship in 1980–81 which served as a charter for private universities. In India, the national government's turn to a market regime in 1991 had a similar role. When state politicians followed up with deregulation and subsidies, they triggered gold rushes. In the central Indian state of Chhattisgarh, after an enabling Act passed in 2002, some 97 private universities appeared within two years; few had decent resources. In the state of Uttar Pradesh, the system was gamed another way. Chaudhary Charan Singh University (formerly Meerut University) became a channel for local businessmen and politicians to set up tax-free enterprises. The sociologist Satendra Kumar observes:

> The result is that CCSU has been reduced from a large and comprehensive public university into a machine that distributes certificates for profit-making private colleges.[7]

As ruling classes abandoned the old class compromises and new-right think tanks and neo-conservative movements demanded tax reductions, all parts of the welfare state came under pressure. Government funding in Australia fell from around 90 per cent of public university budgets in the 1970s to around 42 per cent by 2010. The state still wants teaching and knowledge production from universities, but wants them on the cheap.[8]

A key to the change is that governments began to treat universities, not as cooperating parts of a public education system, but as separate firms, competing in a market and making contracts with the state as service providers. That was consistent with the cultural change in which corporate language and practices became the common sense of the public realm. Education became the making of human capital; public servants became managers; and cut-throat competition was made to appear natural. Public universities were not only surrounded by a cloud of companies trying to make a profit from them, they were also corporatized from within.

The change was not always smooth. In Finland, for instance, there was a brisk political struggle before the public universities were handed over to managerial control in 2009. But they were still handed over. The aggressive dean of a private university law school in the United States got to the nub when he published 'A commercialist manifesto' (which, appropriately, costs $29.95 to read) and declared that 'the university is a business, deal with it'.[9]

We know a lot about how universities have dealt with it. Researchers have published global surveys of the shift to a market regime, and blow-by-blow country narratives from Chile, Britain, Australia, India, and elsewhere. There are close-focus accounts of managerialism and privatization: among the best are Barbara Tuchman's *Wannabe U: Inside the Corporate University*, Margaret Thornton's *Privatising the Public University: The Case of Law*, and Mahmood Mamdani's *Scholars in the Marketplace: The Dilemmas of Neo-liberal Reform at Makerere University*. There are specific studies of the impact on staff and students. I will draw on all these types of research, as well as the stream of publicity put out by corporate universities, and the writings of their defenders and critics.[10]

What enterprise universities sell

Education *in itself* is not a commodity. Education happens in human encounters that depend on care, trust, responsibility and truth, and such encounters cannot be packaged and sold. So what have universities been selling, as students have been transformed into customers?

Basically, access to privileges. The market turn builds on the structures of inequality discussed in Chapter 5, intensifies them and gives them new shapes. Access to a variety of privileges can be sold: to the courses themselves; to the reputation of the institution; to swank buildings and grounds; to favourable teacher/student ratios; to English-language courses; to safe accommodation; and in the background, to qualifications and future advantage in the job market. All these are themes in universities' marketing.

Demanding that students pay tuition fees is the most direct way of selling access, and has become a settled basis of university finances in almost all countries. Typical is the budget of Charles Sturt University, a respected rural university in Australia with several campuses and a staff of about 2000. CSU's revenue in 2014 was 494 million dollars. Of that, 118 million came from fees paid directly, and another 129 million from the government programme known as HELP, which lends fees to students (to be paid back later through the tax system). That is exactly half of the university's total revenue; and CSU is regarded as a public university. I was not surprised to hear, during the 2013 industrial struggle at the University of Sydney, a student remark bitterly that universities now regard students as 'ATMs with legs'.[11]

Fees have been creeping upwards since they were re-introduced in Australia in 1990. In other countries they have been leaping upwards. The resulting mass of student debt has begun to alarm even the hard-line British Treasury. Yet it creates a large corporate interest in the fee system, for the banks and other finance companies that provide the loans. For students, debt becomes a kind of training for a commodified world. They are forced to think of their university time in neoliberal terms, as an investment in human capital with a future economic pay-off.

A crucial fact is that fee-paying became the main mechanism for the *expansion* of higher education. Governments, if they make universities into businesses, can get larger numbers of students without investing public funds. In Brazil and Chile, a mushrooming private college and university sector now accounts for a large majority of higher education students. In India private higher education now has about 50 per cent of enrolments. The Association of African Universities estimated that private institutions had 22 per cent of higher education enrolments across the continent in 2012, and the percentage was rising fast. In China, private universities accounted for nearly 20 per cent of matriculations by 2014, and were complaining about lack of government support.[12]

This trend does not produce a sector like the aristocratic universities. The new private universities sometimes provide a lower-prestige alternative for upper-class youth who did not qualify for the public universities: in Egypt, for instance. More commonly, they provide a lower-fee pathway for lower-middle-class and working-class students looking for jobs in the fraught, insecure labour markets that the market regime produces. For-profit universities in the United States are, substantially, vocational colleges, which often have close connections with employers in their regions. They invite businessmen to help design the courses, and arrange placements and internships. They direct high-pressure marketing to social groups who, in the past, rarely got into the established universities. The curriculum is narrow, and hardly any research is done.[13]

The same logic is now at work on the curriculum of public universities. Courses not making money for the university by enrolling enough students are at risk. Classics and theology are practically gone, despite their vast traditional prestige. Philosophy and foreign languages are in decline (except for English). In every field the specialized, the critical and the unfamiliar are at a discount. Professional programmes too are re-shaped. The bodies of knowledge on which professional education formerly relied are broken down into specific competencies, listed as the intended 'outcomes' of each course. Teacher-education programmes, for instance, have moved away from philosophy and history of education, i.e. reflection on the 'why' of education, towards professional skill sets, i.e. concern with the 'how'. Law programmes, similarly, have moved away from jurisprudence, ethics and the social impact of law towards a focus on practice skills.[14]

The selling of access gradually reshapes the educational process. It places the student in a fundamentally passive role, as consumer of a service, rather than requiring student and teacher to co-create an educational relationship. It also erodes the creativity of teaching. Offering a priced service on the market, university managers are concerned with cost, standardization, and quality control; they want predictable performance and no scandal. The erratic flame of an inspired teacher is not wanted here. Look at the content of the online teacher-training modules that new academic staff are now required to complete. You will be bored out of your mind.

The genius of the market goes beyond selling access to university teaching, to creating customer relations around university research. Research universities long regarded their research findings basically as gifts – to public knowledge, and to other researchers. This changed after the US Congress passed the Bayh-Dole Act in 1980, allowing American universities to make a profit from government-funded research. Since then, concern with 'intellectual property rights' (IPR) has grown enormously.

In any large corporate university nowadays there will be an office with a name like 'Business Engagement and Innovation Services', set up to patent and license discoveries or designs by members of staff. Here is the mission statement of one at a well-known university, helpfully known as Cambridge Enterprise Ltd:

> Our team's mission is to commercialise University knowledge and technology by working with academics, commercial partners, investors, the NHS [National Health Service] and research funders to bring potentially big ideas to market, including by assisting with the formation of new companies and developing licensing opportunities.[15]

Charming disputes sometimes arise with research funders and governments over who owns what share of the IPR in some innovation. Innovation has a specific meaning here: work that produces a product that someone can 'bring to market'. Einstein's work on general relativity was not innovation, clearly. No one has yet worked out how to sell curved space-time.

As the Cambridge Enterprise mission statement shows, universities can now take for granted that knowledge *should* be commodified and sold. This is lucrative for some universities and some areas of research, but not for most. A study of patenting in US universities found that between 1980 and 2000, patents in the biomedical field increased by 2100 per cent, much faster than other fields. By the turn of the century nearly half of university patents were in biomedical science, concentrated in a small group of elite universities.[16]

Patents are not the only way of commodifying knowledge. When Slaughter and Leslie began their research on academic capitalism, they judged consultancy more important. This is the practice where university researchers rent out their skills, whether as expert advisors to corporations and state agencies, or by doing commissioned research projects. Much of this work remains invisible – commercial-in-confidence – so its scale is hard to judge, but there is no reason to think it has died away. In biomedical research, where commissioned research may involve multi-millions of dollars, many jobs depend on it and there is conflict about rights to publish, or suppress, the findings.[17]

The most prestigious way for universities to earn money through research is by winning grants from general funding schemes set up by governments or elite foundations. These do not commodify research directly, but have also been influenced by the market turn. Block grants to universities, which assumed a broad distribution of resources – every researcher was entitled to some part of them – have mostly been replaced by the model of competitive tenders for project-specific grants. This is supposed to reward research excellence. Universities boast of how many their staff win. The staff (operations staff as well as academic staff) spend enormous amounts of time preparing the elaborate grant applications. In Australia, the success rate for project grants in national schemes has been running below 20 per cent, which means that four in five applicants get nothing. The waste of time, energy and expertise is stunning.

And speaking of the genius of markets: the enclosure of knowledge can be used against universities, as well as by them. This has been successfully done by a group of companies that have won control of the 'broadcasting' moment in research. Five publishers now own the journals in which half of the world's research papers in the natural and medical sciences are published. Five own the same proportion in the humanities and social sciences. The paper that documented this situation, 'The oligopoly of academic publishers in the digital era', was published in 2015 in *PLOS One* and is one of that journal's most-read articles. Four transnational corporations appear on both lists. We should know their names: Reed-Elsevier, Wiley-Blackwell, Springer, and Taylor & Francis.[18]

These corporations have been buying up academic journals since the 1960s, and charging for access to their content. Their profits come largely out of university budgets. They have performed a dazzling feat, because they have turned universities into the customers for the universities' own research, and into the bargain get a great deal of free labour from academics as editors, reviewers and authors. The struggle against this cartel, to re-establish open access to research findings, is now a major tension in the knowledge formation.

The managers

Conditions inside universities have changed unevenly under the market regime. In regional public universities, for instance, it is still possible to find old-style administrators with an ethos of public service. But in large urban universities, private universities, and all those oriented to the league tables and the new markets, change has been rapid. Administrators have become managers, and in official statements managers speak, with few exceptions, in a language imported from the corporate world. We now have strategic plans, goals and indicators. We benchmark with competitors. We consult our stakeholders, we pursue excellence, we are committed to our values, we drive change. The language is both vague and complacent; it is designed to conceal more than it reveals.[19]

What it barely conceals is the big shift of power within the organizations. In *The Republic of Learning*, a book I mentioned in the Introduction, the top manager of the University of Melbourne made the barefaced claim that in universities, 'Authority is held collectively by the academic body, represented through an academic board or senate'. This is sheer fiction.[20]

In contemporary universities, major decisions are made within a small group of full-time managers, backed by the corporate managers on their governing councils or boards. In for-profit universities this structure is given from the start, they literally are corporations. Of course the top managers have to negotiate with others: lower managers, academics, governments, unions, other corporations, and even students. But it is in top managers' hands that both executive power and policy-making now rest. I notice that in Australia, during wage bargaining with staff, the managers now call themselves 'The University'.

This group may have an official name such as 'University Senior Team' or 'Senior Executive Group', or it may simply be the informal group in daily discussion with the chief executive, i.e. the president, rector or vice-chancellor. For convenience I will call it the senior management group, SMG. It normally includes a provost or vice-president in charge of academic affairs; a chief financial officer in charge of the cash; and a chief of administration who runs the internal bureaucracy. Depending on the university and the chief executive involved, it may also include vice-presidents or deputy vice-chancellors in charge of research, or fundraising, or international affairs. SMG members each have a personal staff, as well as the larger units they head. They meet each other often. In the American university described in Barbara Tuchman's *Wannabe U* the president's 'cabinet', an expanded SMG, met every Wednesday at 9 am. Informal meetings go on continuously.

Control of finance is vital to them. The major budget decisions are made within the SMG, and other units in the university use their money within these bounds. Other sides of the university's work are also being centralized: as in the wider corporate world, this is increasingly done through on-line systems and the data they generate. Yet managerialism is not only about more tightly controlled routines. It is also about making big decisions – and making them by managerial prerogative. This is particularly visible in 'restructures', where units such as faculties, schools and departments are re-organized, amalgamated or abolished from above, whether they want it or not.

There are vivid accounts of these processes, such as Martin Parker's narrative of events at an elite business school in Europe. This started with the arrival of an aggressive new dean who, with SMG backing, set about a top-down change project. The 'vision' was to become the top business school in Europe. Older staff were defined as dead wood and pushed out. New leaders were brought in, the school was restructured, and new criteria for performance were imposed. To no one's amazement, these were: publishing in elite journals, improving the school's league table position, and creating profitable products. Student fees were increased sharply but funds for teaching programmes were cut. School meetings turned into management presentations. Staff anger was ignored, or dismissed as fear of the new. Parker notes the 'miasma of fear and disgust' that resulted, with a series of resignations by staff.[21]

Who are the managers?

The SMG is recruited from two sources. Those with front-of-house roles (presidents, vice-chancellors, rectors and their deputies) or who supervise research and teaching (e.g. vice-president for research, provost) are almost all recruited from the academic workforce. In rich countries they normally have a PhD, and most have been deans, i.e. middle managers, beforehand. Those with financial, legal or organizational roles (e.g. vice-principal operations, vice-president for development) will have some academic qualification, and perhaps an MBA. Some have been managers in entirely different industries, but more have risen via administrative roles within universities. The careful German study by Krücken and colleagues concluded that the university sector provides most of its own managers. Contrary to what some academics suspect, businessmen have not marched in and occupied universities directly. The SMG resemble corporate managers in other industries because the SMG have actively learnt the corporate culture.[22]

This is a fascinating and little-studied process. The corporations that now cluster around universities vigorously encourage it. EAB (formerly Education Advisory Board), the US consultancy firm valued at $1.55 billion in 2017, holds 'research forums' for university presidents, provosts, chief business officers, and lesser folk, at which it promotes its corporate solutions to 'improve academic efficiency, and grow academic program revenues'. In another enterprise, managers are invited each year to join 'a global network of leaders from the world's best and most ambitious universities' in a World Academic Summit, at which the next year's world rankings will be unveiled. One is not surprised to find that this event is run by *Times Higher Education* (formerly Murdoch group, now private-equity owned) in collaboration with Elsevier, *The Wall Street Journal*, Microsoft, and other public-spirited corporations.[23]

We need to understand the new managers, then, as an emerging social group whose culture is still being formed.

Jill Blackmore and Naarah Sawers are not alone in thinking this involves a re-masculinization of the university, a reaction against the increased presence of women. The managerial takeover installs a form of masculinity that is aggressive, competitive, self-centred and emotionally cold. This is not altered by the fact that some women become vice-chancellors and presidents; it is a myth that female managers are naturally kinder or gentler. To get to the upper levels in the corporate world, women too must 'manage like a man'.[24]

The political scientist Joseph Schwartz argues that university management has now become 'a permanent administrative class'. Certainly, it is now unusual to be anything but a manager once one has become a manager. There is a career path: a dean can become a provost, a provost can become a president, and a president can rise from running a lowly college to running a bigger and richer one. But there is a danger of exaggerating the coherence of the group. Jonathan Jansen's interviews with vice-chancellors in South Africa suggest a more fractured and uncertain group, admittedly in a period of crisis. Divisions between managements became obvious during the 2018 university strike in Britain.[25]

At the top levels, university managers are now very well paid – five to ten times higher than most academic and operations staff and enormously more than casualized or outsourced workers. There is now a corporate-style practice, too, of paying upper managers cash bonuses each year when 'targets' in their areas of responsibility are met. (Meeting the targets is actually accomplished by the work of rank-and-file staff, who do not get bonuses.)

Senior managers, as well as being the key decision-makers, are the big winners in the new order. An ethical problem here? Few managers seem troubled. Neoliberal economics plays a useful role, explaining that top people's incomes are determined by The Market. University councils and boards sometimes quote that explanation to excuse the million-dollar packages they have agreed to.

As I noted in Chapter 3, an intellectual workforce is hard to control. Managers have to work at this. There is still old-fashioned bullying, as Martin Parker's business-school narrative illustrates. Union branches spend a lot of energy fighting distressing individual cases of bullying. Yet the most striking thing about the new corporate management is its love of *indirect* ways to control staff. Michael Power describes this in the admirable book I have already mentioned, *The Audit Society*. The ancient technical device of auditing has morphed, in the neoliberal era, into a system of self-policing. The result is a baroque proliferation of performance-management schemes, obligatory reporting systems, and metrics. This is not small beer. A recent estimate for Britain suggests that 8 per cent of the university teaching budget in that country is spent on 'quality assurance' measures.[26]

In wealthy universities, computer systems now regulate not only the use of money but also student enrolment, staff career progression, and – notably – teaching. All courses must be fitted into online templates. The templates standardize lecture timetables, the use of lecture halls and laboratories, prescribed readings, everyday communication with students, required assessment and recording of marks. These management-controlled systems are invisible to the public and mostly invisible to students, yet in the last twenty years have become a central feature of academic and operations work in universities.

Ben Williamson, who has closely studied digitization in Britain, notes how the drive for the 'smarter university' – this mad term is actually in use – brings an array of profit-making companies and consultancies into core areas of university work even in the public sector. Computerizing the work of administration and teaching generates 'big data', now being coordinated by government to support its own market agenda. This creates strong pressure for standardization of practices, to produce data and allow management at a distance, and so shrinks the space for creative and engaged teaching.

As a bonus, the close involvement with digital-economy companies reinforces the learning of corporate culture by university managers.[27]

In relation to the academic and operations staff, the auditing regime embeds distrust. No university worker is trusted just to get on with their job and do it competently. Individuals as well as departments and faculties are required to set formal goals, evaluate themselves, and report their compliance and their outcomes. But this does not produce a closer relationship between managers and staff. In fact it produces greater social distance, just as digitization does. The *isolation* of senior managers from rank-and-file workers is now a key feature of the university scene. Active academic and operations workers can go for years without seeing a member of their SMG, except on a podium or a website. The distrust goes both ways.

Managements seem to have little gut awareness of the level of stress and the potential for anger among university workers, especially in the non-core workforce with low salaries, low security, little power, and low job satisfaction. That is partly because the top managers are now so isolated. But it is also because they are committed to public fantasies about university life.

Telling lies about universities

In the corner of the old quadrangle at the University of Sydney, from the 1920s there was a jacaranda tree. It was famous because it blossomed about the time graduation ceremonies were held, so generations of graduands have been photographed in their robes under the purple tree. Backed by the mock-gothic building in golden sandstone, it made a great picture, so it was frequently shown in the university's corporate advertising. Around 2013 this advertising featured a tutorial or discussion group of students, sitting in a semi-circle on the grass in front of the jacaranda tree in full bloom, talking earnestly together in bright Sydney sunshine. Marvellous image!

But the picture was lying to us. No class or discussion group is allowed to convene on the quadrangle lawn. It is therefore redundant to observe that jacarandas in Sydney bloom mainly in November, after tutorials are over. The tree died in 2016.

This is a small example, which I noticed because I was fond of that tree. The point is, this kind of falsification has become routine. Every managerial university now puts out a cloud of imagery, text and sound intended to misrepresent the way things really are.

In the first study of image-making by Australian universities, Colin Symes noted how prospectuses resembled a cross between a teen magazine and a tourist brochure. Today's online sites carry this style forward. If the university has a bit of gothic architecture, it will be featured; second choice is a classical column; third choice is a very modern building with lots of glass, not brick. Some of the imagery shows young people with back-packs and hiking boots in splendid landscapes – the University of Tasmania assures families that what really counts in choosing a university is the 'lifestyle'. Collages are common, a show of highlights. Everyone is smiling. There is never any stress, disappointment or grinding hard work on our lovely campus![28]

The websites are part of a process of turning universities into spectacle. There is growing expenditure on showy buildings, if possible designed by fashionable architects. The league tables are designed for publicity, and each year university managements pick out the results that suit them and trumpet their vacuous claim to excellence on Facebook, Twitter, and media releases. Many have adopted a one-line slogan, which they constantly repeat in advertisements, announcements and banners. Some are monumentally silly. The University of New South Wales, a perfectly respectable university, proclaims as its philosophy: 'Never Stand Still'. Whether they are always running for the tram, or dancing the jitterbug, history doesn't relate.

Putting out a cloud of misrepresentation is work, most of which is done in public-relations units attached to central management, with names like 'University Communications'. In Chile, it has been estimated, advertising took 2 per cent of the higher education budget by 2002. The University of Western Sydney paid consultants a shovel-full of money to change its name to Western Sydney University (this is true), and then budgeted 30 million dollars for advertising the new image; all that could possibly be said about this is in an extremely funny video by the comedian Aamer Rahman.[29]

Managements also direct propaganda at their own staff. In the 'staff news' bulletins that arrive weekly in everyone's inboxes, there are more pictures of grown-ups but everyone is still grinning fit to bust, unless they are peering through a microscope at a deadly germ. Happy groups of staff have just been awarded a prize or gained promotion, or are gathered to witness the university president opening a new building. There are never any setbacks, sackings or strikes on our lovely campus!

It is easy to laugh at this, but continuous distortion is a serious matter. The expansion of control mechanisms requires staff constantly to display their compliance and performance to managers. Meanwhile the managers have to display the university's compliance and performance to governments and ratings agencies. The result is a spectacular growth of fake accountability, where an *appearance* of compliance and good performance is created.[30]

Managements have led the way, gaming external evaluation systems. In 1992 the high-stakes Research Assessment Exercise was introduced in Britain, elaborating earlier attempts to rank departments for the quality of their research, and giving funds to universities accordingly. It was followed by a famous outbreak of poaching as universities tried to lure productive researchers from other universities, to boost their own scores and depress their rivals'. Managers pressure researchers to publish only in top-ranked journals. This practice does not improve the quality of research, nor place knowledge in the hands of people who need it. It can improve a particular university's score in the short run. In the long run, since the rankings are relative and the other universities are trying to game the system in the same way, the net result is futility.

Internal accountability systems too are constantly gamed. They *have* to be, or the work of the university would grind to a halt. In order to get on with their jobs and protect their students, the staff delay making reports, forget formal requirements, lose unnecessary demands, massage administrative data, and pretend compliance in other ways. It is childish, and no one likes doing it. But evading intrusive and time-wasting management requirements has become a necessary skill for university workers.[31]

No contemporary management reveals a major policy without declaring that it has engaged in Wide Consultation. The consultation may be an online survey, visits to department or faculty meetings, 'town hall' forums where a manager fronts a lecture theatre, or briefings to which middle and junior managers are called, notionally representing their units. These devices have replaced actual decision-making by voting in constituted bodies, and they are normally spurious. The policy choices are made by opaque processes within the senior management group.

Image-polishing usually goes together with lying by concealment, and this cries out for attention. The British academic Marina Warner, who resigned on principle, quotes one of the gagging orders imposed on a colleague when given a pay-out:

> You agree that you have not and undertake that you will not (either directly or indirectly) make, publish or otherwise communicate any disparaging or derogatory

> comments whether in writing or otherwise and whether or not they are considered by you to be true, concerning the University or any Associated Entity, or any of its or their present or former officers or employees.[32]

Warner notes there were more than *five thousand* recorded non-disclosure agreements in British universities in the three years to 2010.

It is not just criticism from retrenched staff that is covered up. Corruption happens in universities and is almost certainly increasing as the sector becomes more profit-focussed. Very few cases are publicly acknowledged or referred to police. The usual solution is a quiet retirement, sometimes a pay-off. Highly embarrassing statistics, such as the proportion of undergraduate teaching that is done by casualized or adjunct staff, are concealed. Laura Pulido notes how the management of the University of Southern California made it almost impossible to get data about tenure decisions, when challenged about bias against women and people of colour. Universities' publicity units rarely give any hard detail about current industrial disputes, though they put out management spin. Published financial reports from universities are usually so generalized that they give little information about real conditions or current problems. Some annual reports I have seen from large universities are little more than advertising brochures.[33]

Why worry about all this? Advertising is always deceptive and everyone knows it. Managers in other industries treat their workforce like mushrooms. Corporations cheat and lie, that is what they are for. As an eighteenth-century Lord Chancellor of England remarked, corporations have neither bodies to be kicked, nor souls to be damned; they therefore do as they like.[34]

But a *university* cannot do this, because a university does have a soul. Our business is truth. That is the basis of the university's legitimacy, its claim to respect and, to be materialistic, its claim on public funds, tax relief and endowments. In Chapter 1 I discussed the importance of truthful practice for the research-based knowledge formation. Everyone who does research knows how difficult it is to establish truth, and everyone who teaches knows the pains of learning about it. But all know that we have to make the effort.

Maelstrom reconsidered

Few staff or students in universities wanted the changes mapped in this chapter. The cascade began because universities' circumstances changed, with the resurgence of corporate power on a world scale, rising pressure against autonomous development strategies in the global South, and ferocious attacks on the tax-supported public sector in the global North. It is impossible to tell how much of the outcome was due to financial crisis and how much due to ideology; the course of events differed from country to country. But the direction of change was similar. As the pressure rose, university managers and market-oriented governments negotiated fee-based funding for universities, corporate-style restructures, and commodification of research. Like Dr Faust in his bargain with the Devil, universities got short-term solutions to their problems and were then stuck with the long-term consequences.

Critics often picture the market regime as a tightly-knit economic system and the neoliberal university as a well-oiled corporate machine. I think both are messier than those images suggest, more incoherent and conflict-ridden. Indeed the violence of the global market regime and the oppressiveness of the managerial university are largely due to their incoherence, to the need of managers, plutocrats and generals to *impose* their order on a messy and resistant reality. They often get it wrong.

In the market transformation of the university world there have been many false moves. In one case determined in 2005, and another in 2014, the Supreme Court of India cracked down on dozens of private universities that lacked proper buildings and trained teachers, failed to do research, or otherwise violated the national guidelines. In 1998 the managers of the public University of Melbourne, my alma mater, launched a private college to exploit the Melbourne brand, called Melbourne University Private Ltd. Within three years the fantasy collapsed, and the real university had to take over its property.[35]

The result of the market turn is by no means the free, efficient competition that neoliberal ideology exalts. A number of analysts point out that universities are actually in pseudo-markets, where all the terms of competition are set by the state. The managerial university is at best a hybrid institution, in Hugo Radice's phrase 'a simulated private enterprise'.[36]

Contrary to neoliberal doctrine, market logic does not lead to creativity and diversity. In education it normally leads to convergence on the market leader. In the university world this is a very strong effect: everyone would like to look like Harvard. Sean Sturm and Stephen Turner, discussing disputes at the University of Auckland in Aotearoa New Zealand, observe that a university in the global periphery in pursuit of 'excellence' *must* follow imported models. Market pressure produces what they call provincialism – i.e. extraversion – and prevents genuine originality. The 'Bologna process' that began in 1999, intended to make European higher education competitive with the United States, became the largest exercise in standardization that the university world has ever seen.[37]

Looking at university transformations on a world scale it is hard to believe they reveal market-driven efficiency and improvement. Mahmood Mamdani's very detailed account of privatization at Makerere University is illuminating. Change here was enabled by government and senior management, egged on by World Bank consultants: so far, the familiar story. But in a low-wage economy, privatization was a quick way for academic staff to augment their salaries. During the 1990s a free-for-all occurred with rival departments and faculties pushing hard for fee-paying private students, poaching enrolments from each other and selling services to each other, marginalizing research and replacing disciplinary courses with low-level vocational programmes. In China, by contrast, marketization has been controlled throughout by the party-state, more easily because a proportion of the university managers are always Party members. Driven by the state's agenda, the result has been a two-tier academic system, with the elite research universities teaching in English and entering global competition, the mass of universities competing in local labour markets.[38]

Broadly speaking, the market turn has transformed universities from being a cooperating set of public sector agencies, to being a hybrid and fragmented industry of contractors to the state. The industry has grown. It has delivered profits to its managers and owners, profits to the cloud of corporations that now service and exploit universities, and ideological gain to those groups who benefit from the corporate economy generally. It delivers export earnings from overseas student fees to some governments (mainly in rich English-speaking countries), and supplies expensive vocational courses to many economies.

The market turn has achieved these results at some cost. Inequality among universities has risen, and their role in generating social inequality has been reinforced. The idea that universities exist to serve the public good survives, but is now overshadowed – in policy and publicity – by the logic of private benefit. The industry increasingly separates research from teaching, undermining the intellectual rationale of the modern university.[39]

Inequality of power and income within the institutions has risen, and democratic means of decision-making have declined or been abolished. For large groups of staff there is increased insecurity, stress, and what Rosalind Gill calls the 'hidden injuries of neo-liberal academia': work intensification, fear and shame.[40]

Distrust between staff and managements has grown, and open conflict has become more common. Tightening internal controls, especially those imposed by digital systems, narrows the space for creativity and invention in teaching. The commodification of research findings and publication outlets undermines the knowledge commons created from research-based knowledge. The outsourcing and casualization of labour leads towards a crisis of sustainability for the university workforce. The enterprise university distorts reality in its marketing, its manipulation of staff, its gaming of audit and its suppression of information: short-term answers that in the long term devastate universities' credibility and commitment to truth.

The costs are experienced daily by the university workforce. Low-key opposition constantly emerges. It bubbles up in sceptical staffroom talk, in the gaming of reporting systems, in minimal compliance with management demands. Gina Anderson, who has studied these manoeuvres in Australian universities, speaks of the 'weapons of the weak' and the 'local tactics' that show scepticism and sardonic humour. The situation is far from amusing when capable, creative staff can only protest by leaving their jobs. Marina Warner, mentioned a few pages ago, was one. María Cristina Laverde Toscano, a senior academic in Colombia, was another. She had built up a research centre for interdisciplinary social science at the Universidad Central and edited a very impressive journal for critical studies called *Nómadas*. Her position was undermined by the university management's turn to competition, metrics, and conservative conceptions of disciplines, and she too found no alternative but resigning.[41]

Opposition eventually moves into the public realm. I began this book with the strike at the University of Sydney in 2013. As I was writing it in 2017 there was another, for similar reasons. In 2009 there was a mass strike in French universities against market-regime measures the Sarkozy government was trying to introduce. In Chile, where privatization has been extreme, mass protests by university students broke out in 2011, culminating in a Santiago demonstration of nearly a million people. In 2015–16 a sharp conflict arose at the University of Newcastle in Britain, following management's heavy-handed attempt to improve its league table position by imposing performance demands on staff. After nine months of dispute, as industrial action began, management backed down. But in 2018 there was an embittered national strike over the university pension scheme in England.[42]

Detailed critiques of the market regime and managerialism have been multiplying, and growing more sophisticated. Managers and policymakers rarely pay attention to these critiques, preferring to dismiss them as hopeless nostalgia or conspiracy theory from ill-tempered Jeremiahs.[43]

Others may hear them. If they do, they will want critics to point out a better path for universities. So, what alternatives have there been? I give a messy, but I hope interesting, answer in the next chapter.

Chapter 7

Universities of hope

Higher education has a colourful history with many alternative models and many reform movements. In this chapter I introduce some of them and reflect on their lessons. There is a great deal of *practical* experience in doing things differently from the corporate model.

The European research university, it is worth remembering, was created by a great reform movement. The mediaeval university too was the product of bold invention and wide synthesis. In its formative stages, teachers like Peter Abelard in Paris were regarded as dangerous near-heretics. Catholic Europe drew from its contacts with Arabic, Greek, Berber and Turkish-speaking cultures, which were in touch with farther civilizations in Asia and Africa. Along the trade routes with the spice and silk came the texts of Aristotle and the formula for gunpowder, chess, place-based numerals – the zero possibly came from South-east Asia – linguistics, philosophy, geography, and more. We still use Arabic and Greek names for fields like algebra, chemistry and physics.[1]

Famous and well-endowed higher education centres existed in the Arab world, especially in Baghdad and Cairo. India had great centres of Buddhist learning at Nalanda and Vikramashila. Confucian China had an elaborate state system of higher learning and produced innovative science. Many societies did not have formal institutions of higher learning, but still had organized ways of handling knowledge – spiritual, environmental, medical, and more. An example is the role of elders in Australian Aboriginal societies, responsible for specific bodies of knowledge and for introducing the next generation to them.[2]

No single knowledge formation exhausts the human possibilities of knowing. Societies have many needs for knowledge and generate an enormous range of temporary and local knowledge projects, as well as elaborated ones. Universities produce and hold knowledge, but also need to learn from what is around them.

Histories of invention

As European colonizers spread their college model around the world, connections with other knowledge formations were made. I have mentioned the British East India Company's experiment with Muslim and Hindu colleges in Bengal. The main impulse for innovation came from the colonized themselves. A group of prominent local men including Rammohan Roy launched the secular Hindoo College in Bengal in 1817 (later called Presidency College, recently Presidency University). A comparable but firmly religious initiative was the Aligarh complex in northern India. Its leading figure was Sayyid Ahmad Khan, who allied with the British to launch a modernization project among Indian Muslims. The college he set up became the present Aligarh Muslim University in 1920.

These colleges moved towards a European model, but others were oppositional in content and pedagogy. A notable example was the *Visva-Bharati* college set up by Rabindranath Tagore in Bengal (see Box 1), who boldly proposed it as a meeting-place between civilizations.

1 Visva-Bharati

Rabindranath Tagore was the son of a landlord family in Bengal, who came of age at the high tide of British imperial power in India. Sent off to become a lawyer, he dropped out and became a poet instead – to some effect, he was awarded the Nobel Prize in 1913, and became India's most famous writer. He was sharply critical of the colonial universities set up by the British, for disregarding Indian culture and lacking a spirit of enquiry.

Tagore launched an experimental school on his family's land to provide a model of education closer to the people and to nature. From the village school grew the project for a college, which opened in 1921. It was started with three departments, all drawing on rich Indian traditions: Fine Arts, Music, and Indology (including language and history; later Tibetan and Chinese were added). The offerings gradually expanded, and students came from all over India. Among them were two people later famous: the great film-maker Satyajit Ray, and prime minister Indira Gandhi.

The name Visva-Bharati combines terms for Universe and the Goddess of Learning. The ambition was to create a meeting-place for civilizations – European, Indian, east Asian and Islamic – a kind of world university. It was to be a place for knowledge production as well as teaching. Tagore wanted to recruit people active in 'research, invention or creative activity', and valued science and technology as well as spirituality. While travelling he tried to recruit scholars as well as raise funds, and some did come from overseas, for instance from the Sorbonne.

There were difficulties from the start. The project was under-funded, the facilities poor, and Tagore struggled to raise money from private donors. By the end of the 1930s Visva-Bharati was in financial crisis. There was a personality cult around the founder, who provided great inspiration, but was often away, and was not a good organizer. It was difficult to recruit qualified staff, given financial problems and rural location.

Yet Visva-Bharati survived. It was brought into the public university system in 1951, after Indian independence. It currently has a handsome website with pictures of both traditional crafts and rows of computers, and on the home page a quotation, of course, from Rabindranath Tagore.[3]

Equally bold was the design for an international research centre for Islamic knowledge in Iran. This was planned in the 1970s by the sociologist-theologian Ali Shariati on the basis of the reform institute *Hosseiniyeh Ershad*. Shariati was thrown into prison, and the institute was closed by the neocolonial regime of the Shah, before much could be done. But Shariati's 'Practical Plan' survived and is available in translation. It is a fascinating document, proposing a strong research and documentation agenda, an imaginative and democratic curriculum, and an inclusive pedagogy with wide public outreach.[4]

Perhaps the most dramatic example of an oppositional university was the Flying University in Poland, a country colonized alternately from Russia and Germany (see Box 2). It is an astonishing story of devotion to intellectual life and education under three authoritarian governments. Its scale was limited, and it was hurt by internal disputes. But the story demonstrates what can be done with popular support.

2 The Flying University

In the late nineteenth century the Russian empire, which then ruled most of Poland, cracked down on universities and tried to Russify them. In Warsaw a remarkable response occurred.

Local people began to hold study circles in apartments and houses. In 1885–86 these were organized into a systematic programme, with a coordinating board, financed by fees from students. They became known as the 'Flying University' because the classes had to move around to dodge the police. But the surveillance had one benefit: the police archives preserved the curriculum for historians! The courses covered social and natural sciences, mathematics, humanities, and education. Around 1890 there were about a thousand students, many of them women aiming to become school teachers.

The academic standard seems to have been high; many lecturers were academics from official universities, moonlighting at the risk of their careers. One of their students was Maria Sklodowska, who as Marie Curie went on to win two Nobel Prizes in science.

There was conflict in the group however, a split, and reorganization on looser lines. In this form the Flying University continued underground until the revolution of 1905. At that time the illegal university became the legal 'Association of Scientific Courses'. In 1920, with Polish independence, it became the Free Polish University.

In 1939 the Nazis invaded Poland, closed all universities and began murdering Polish intellectuals. Even under this terrible repression, some underground high school and university courses were run, in Warsaw and Poznan.

When the Red Army crushed the Nazis and installed a communist regime in Poland, the public universities were restored in a devastated country. There was some attempt to widen the intake to include children of the working class. But the curriculum was kept under tight political control.

The response was to run illicit lectures and study circles focussed on the forbidden topics – social science and history. In 1977–78 the Flying University was revived as an underground 'Society for Academic Courses'. In its first year some 120 lectures were delivered, with audiences totalling five thousand. Support came from academics in the official universities and from the Church. The group began publishing papers, and international support was found. Police harassment followed, and violence from the regime's youth organization; but the study circles continued into the 1980s.[5]

During the 1950s and 1960s, in both the global North and newly independent countries of the South, university expansion was driven by a wave of public investment. A whole generation of new universities was built. Some followed old models, but many experimented with organization and teaching (see Box 3). For twenty years or so, they were the key source of new practices in world higher education.

3 Greenfields

In Britain the postwar foundations were called 'greenfields' universities, built in concrete, steel and glass on the fringes of industrial and commercial cities (the

(continued)

(continued)

University of East Anglia was built on the local golf course). They multiplied and opened quickly. In Britain, seven new universities were opened between 1961 and 1965. In the United States, the University of California alone opened seven new campuses between 1958 and 1965. Many newly independent countries created universities to provide a national focus. Though India already had a substantial higher education system, the parliament established Jawaharlal Nehru University in this role in 1966.

The greenfields universities were imagined as components of national or statewide university systems, not as isolated institutions. They were usually located where planners identified a growing student population, and they were expected to collaborate with each other and with older universities. Governments wanted the existing knowledge formation extended, not challenged. Yet the greenfields universities were intended to bring in new populations of students. Their founders intended to blow away the cobwebs from university life, serve the public interest and stimulate public debate.

I taught in three of them: Flinders University in Adelaide, Macquarie University in Sydney, and the University of California at Santa Cruz. By contrast with the older 'sandstone' universities where I began an academic career, they were consciously open to experiment. There was a widespread attempt to break down barriers between staff and students with more participatory teaching. The map of knowledge was re-thought, with cross-disciplinary programmes in new fields like urban studies and environmental science.

A famous example is the Open University in Britain, launched in the 1960s by a modernizing Labour government. Open University became celebrated for its television programmes, its far-flung tutorials, and its book series designed to overcome distant students' lack of libraries – some so good that they became standard references in new fields of knowledge.[6]

Being entirely dependent on state funding, the greenfields universities were vulnerable when governments shifted towards a market regime. The institutions have survived, but the collective élan, the sense of being the cutting-edge of a great democratic reform, has gone.

The radical social movements of the 1960s and 1970s, in which students were very prominent, produced a lot of educational experimentation. Some of it was inside existing universities in the global North, such as the Free Speech Movement at the University of California in Berkeley. Activism also developed in more humble institutions like the City College of New York, where a famous strike happened in 1969 (see Box 4). The most devastating experience, however, was in Mexico City. A student mobilization in 1968 in defence of political reform and university autonomy was confronted by an authoritarian government. A rally in the Tlatelolco district was surrounded by the army and a massacre followed, with possibly 300 students and onlookers killed.

Social movements also worked outside the state, setting up autonomous education projects such as the Freedom Schools in the southern United States. This was the strategy followed by an international Free University movement that began in the mid-1960s. Their idea was to provide movement bases for a range of loosely linked, self-managed courses of study which operated under no limits except people's energy. With a strong commitment to new-left ideas of participatory democracy, these projects produced imaginative curricula and sometimes intense learning experiences.

4 Free Universities and liberated zones

In 1971 Jane Lichtman drove her van across the United States, visiting 43 states to conduct a survey of Free Universities. She counted 110 of them, with many thousands of participants in total. Her report *Bring Your Own Bag*, a little-known but important document on experimental universities, is available online.

One of the largest was the Midpeninsula Free University in California. This ran for about five years in public spaces and participants' living rooms. It produced a splendid magazine and a lively counter-cultural experience, and provided a base for anti-war activism. Its work is recorded in an excellent online archive. The Free University in Sydney, which rented its own premises, tried to combine activism and research, and had more links to the labour movement. (Confession: I was involved in this one.)

Free Universities worked across multiple fields of knowledge. Lichtman classifies the courses into three groups: skills, science, and head trips. Free U Sydney ran a course on Gödel's theorem as well as a research programme on class structure in Australia. All Free Universities were based on voluntary labour and none found a stable base. Midpeninsula was wrecked by a left-sectarian takeover, others lost momentum and faded away.[7]

Free Universities did not expand access much beyond the social groups already represented in universities, but in some mainstream institutions access became the focus. A major struggle developed at City College of New York in Harlem, part of the city's free public university system (CUNY). The students were mainly White, though the college sat in an African-American and Puerto Rican neighbourhood – Harlem was, indeed, a famous centre of Black culture. In 1965 the college set up an access programme called SEEK, and gathered a talented group of teachers for it, including the poet Adrienne Rich. In the poem 'Diving into the Wreck', written after four years teaching in SEEK, she said:

> I came to see the damage that was done
> And the treasures that prevail.

The programme did try to connect teaching with the treasures of marginalized cultures, and create treasures of engagement and solidarity.

Around them, the social conflicts of the American 1960s boiled up, and in 1969 a student/staff strike and occupation at CCNY followed, closing the college for two weeks and demanding a school of Third World Studies and racial equality in admissions. The city government conceded open admissions but not the new school. The SEEK programme was saved – indeed it became central to making open admissions work, with 3500 students in the autumn of 1969.

The SEEK programme was the venue for inventive, engaged teaching and curriculum-making, discovering and circulating resources from Black and Hispanic culture and original writing by staff and students. Intense discussions about language (e.g. the status of Black English), power and racial oppression spilled from staffrooms into classes and the even more intense space of the strike. The collective and emotional dimensions of education came strongly to the surface. For perhaps ten years the programme was a kind of liberated zone, a remarkable site of knowledge production. It became widely known, and sharpened ideas about what inclusion in higher education really demands.[8]

Contemporaries

In the decade after 2000, left-wing governments came to power in a number of Latin American countries. The labour and popular movements that swelled this 'pink tide' rejected the market agenda and subjection to international capital. They were critical of existing universities' connection with class privilege. They could draw on a regional tradition of *educación popular*, education for the people, and the work of intellectuals such as Paulo Freire, Ivan Illich, and the creators of Liberation Theology. The new governments launched a number of new universities to widen access and reform teaching (Box 5).

5 Pink tide

The Workers Party government in Brazil installed by the election of Lula as president in 2002 used its direct power to set up a group of new universities. They included a University of Latin American Integration, teaching in Spanish as well as Portuguese; an Afro-Brazilian university, to serve the dramatically under-represented Black population; and universities in frontier regions. At the same time the government introduced quotas and scholarships in existing universities to boost the numbers from under-represented groups. There were also private universities serving African and regional communities, universities based on indigenous knowledge or spiritism, and a decentralized university intended to serve social movements.

The Chávez government in Venezuela also confronted the social exclusions in the old university system. Its main vehicle was the Bolivarian University of Venezuela, practically a parallel university system, launched in 2003 as part of an 'education for all' drive. It was based on a radical decentralization, scattering 1800 classrooms, *aldeas universitarias* (university villages), in community centres across the country. Support programmes were established for people not yet qualified for entry. Pedagogy was focussed on team projects based on fieldwork. The proposed role of teachers was not authority but *acompañamiento*, 'accompanying' students in their learning. The curriculum was to be defined by social needs, such as legal reform or environment.

Fast, large-scale change agendas can expect to hit problems, and these encountered many. Outside the government sector, the alternative universities in Brazil operated on a shoestring and some relied on volunteer staff. They did not offer recognized diplomas, so there was no flood of poor students coming in. The Venezuelan project too faced problems of recognition: many academic staff lacked higher qualifications, the Bolivarian University published little research, and the quality of teaching was uneven. In both countries the older university system sat alongside the new, with more prestige. In due course the Venezuelan government tried to integrate the systems, but this faced opposition from the older universities, citing 'standards'. And, eventually, the tide ebbed; progressive governments lost power in much of the continent in the 2010s.[9]

Under the terrible pressures of colonial conquest – massacres, epidemics, uprooting from homeland – the knowledge systems of many indigenous societies were badly disrupted. But not obliterated: there was great resilience.

In recent years, indigenous political movements have revived a concern with place-based knowledge, triggering changes in the university world (see Box 6). One of the earliest initiatives was the First Nations University of Canada; others were founded in Nicaragua, Mexico, Colombia, Ecuador, Peru and Bolivia. In 2008 seven institutions set up an association, now known as RUIICAY, the Network of Indigenous, Intercultural and Community Universities of Abya Yala (an indigenous name for the Americas). RUIICAY has compiled a statement of principles as well as looking at legal problems, accreditation and indicators. It defines the central elements as: ancestral knowledge; a decolonizing paradigm; and overcoming the rupture between theory and practice.[10] There are now indigenous-knowledge universities, colleges, and programmes within universities, not only across Abya Yala but also in the Pacific, Africa, South Asia, and even far-north Europe among the Sami people.

6 Ocean, mountain, indigenous knowledge

In 1997 the University of the South Pacific, located in Fiji and supported by a number of island states, opened the Oceania Centre for Arts and Culture. Its director was Epeli Hau'ofa, one of the region's most influential and multi-talented writers; the tale is told in his book *We Are the Ocean*. It came after fifteen years of academic debate about a proposal to open a cultural centre as a nostalgia-driven tourist attraction.

The Oceania Centre is very different. Hau'ofa was acutely aware of the cultural and social losses that had occurred, not only under colonialism but also when post-independence island societies were swept into the circuits of global capitalism and development aid. Indigenous culture was not preserved by nostalgia; it had to be freshly created in new conditions. And that is what the Oceania Centre set about doing. With few resources it became a busy site for painters, sculptors, musicians and performing artists.

The movement for Māori culture and education in Aotearoa New Zealand, called Kaupapa Māori, is more widely known. One of its activists, Linda Tuhiwai Smith, wrote the classic text *Decolonizing Methodologies*, showing how indigenous communities become the authors, not the objects, of research. The movement, with state funding, has built the multi-site institution Te Whare Wananga o Awanuiarangi, offering both university and technical college programmes in distinctive Māori forms since the 1990s.

Several countries in South America have proposed higher education based on the distinctive *cosmovisiónes* of Andean cultures, their integral outlook on the universe and life. The republic of Bolivia, under its first indigenous president Evo Morales, set up the Indigenous University of Bolivia with three campuses (for different language groups), which awarded their first degrees in 2014. It has also tried to bring a decolonizing perspective into teachers' colleges, *normales*, serving the school system.

A careful study of the Bolivian *normales* by Mieke Lopes Cardozo shows some of the difficulties. It is hard to systematize indigenous knowledge to create a generally accepted curriculum. Not all indigenous parents want it: many want Spanish, modernity and economic advancement for their children. There are problems in a government demanding de-colonial education while using soldiers and tear gas to drive development projects through. Conservative media attack the indigenous curriculum as socially divisive, and higher education staff themselves may resist. But projects of this kind continue to emerge around the world.[11]

Indigenous-knowledge projects usually engage with the dominant knowledge formation – one of RUIICAY's principles is 'scientificity' – but intend more than adding footnotes to it. They assert, to use a phrase from the Mexican discussions, an educational sovereignty in their own land. Indigenous knowledge is connected with land and sea, and with the whole structure of indigenous society, in ways regulated by indigenous law.[12]

This is one of the most creative and genuinely challenging reform movements on the university scene at present. It tests the dominant knowledge formation, as well as confronting the neoliberal 'intellectual property' regime. The movement brings new resources into university research and teaching, and shows practical ways of crossing epistemic boundaries.

Without doubt the most resilient model of higher education is the advanced schools of Islamic knowledge. They are more than a thousand years old; they have survived changes of dynasties, the violence of European colonization, and postcolonial dependency and conflict. Islam has no priesthood. It has an enormously important intellectual tradition. Its clerics are traditionally scholars who acquire prestige and influence through their learning.

For the last hundred and fifty years there has been controversy over the relation between Islamic knowledge and 'Western' science, and about the role of the scholar-clerics, the *ulama*, in modernization. It was a main concern of the famous critic and activist al-Afghani, at the peak of European imperial power. Debates about this balance, and about the sustainability of Islamic science, have continued ever since. Not just in words, because these are practical questions too. Many universities in Muslim-majority countries have to solve every day the problems of running technoscience and religious scholarship in the same institution (see Box 7). Their experience is a resource for any institution that faces the problem of connecting knowledge formations – which is to say, all universities today.[13]

7 Al-Azhar

The most famous centre of Islamic learning grew around the principal mosque in the new city of Cairo, founded by the Shiite Fatimid dynasty in the tenth century CE. Later, under Egypt's Mamluk rulers, the informal schools associated with the mosque became the international centre of Sunni scholarship, drawing students from the Maghreb to the west, the upper Nile to the south, and the Arab east. They studied Qur'anic interpretation, *fiqh* or Islamic jurisprudence (which is broader than the European discipline of 'law'), and a variety of subjects including philosophy and mathematics. Al-Azhar became known for a widely inclusive approach to Islamic scholarship.

When Egypt shook off British rule in the mid-twentieth century, it faced the same dilemma as other postcolonial states, needing a higher education system as part of a modernization drive. But Egypt already had al-Azhar, as well as some secular universities. In 1961 the military regime headed by Jamal 'Abd al-Nasir brought al-Azhar into an expanded state education system, adding faculties of natural science, medicine and technology. It left the Islamic religious studies, and the connection with the ancient and prestigious mosque. In fact the regime sought to use this prestige for the nation-building project.

State funding allowed al-Azhar to grow on a massive scale; it now claims 500 000 students, across multiple campuses, and some overseas franchises. It has its own admissions system and a large group of affiliated high schools. Research on access shows that al-Azhar's intake is the most democratic in the Egyptian higher education sector, with more rural students, more from low-income families, and – strikingly – more women (but with gender-segregated programmes).

The modern al-Azhar University is thus a state agency of an unusual kind. The preamble to the 1961 law declared:

> Islam, in its original reality, does not make a distinction between the science of religion (*din*) and the science of this world (*dunya*). Islam is indeed a social religion.

This is indeed an Islamic tradition, and al-Azhar is a remarkable example of holding together in one institution what others see as different forms of knowledge. It has not been simple. The close teacher/pupil relationship in mosque-based learning could not be reproduced in the new professional courses. The teaching of Islamic knowledge had to be modified for a larger, more secular student body, using introductory textbooks rather than the difficult classical texts.

The relationship with the state has created difficulties for al-Azhar, which played an ambiguous role in the 'Arab spring' rising, and had a tense relationship with the Islamist government that came to power in 2012. The university's managers have supported the current military regime, which in turn has put pressure on the university to censor its religious teaching, to combat extremism. This has divided the university's staff, and threatens al-Azhar's prized position as an authoritative site of religious scholarship.[14]

Setting up independent learning and research centres is an old strategy in labour movements. In the early twentieth century radical unions created Labor Colleges with a specifically socialist curriculum. In the later twentieth century a number of unions, and most large union confederations, established their own research units. There is a Global Labour University backed by the International Labour Organization; its teaching began in 2004. This is not autonomous, however. It is a network in existing universities, providing master's degree courses for union activists.[15]

8 Autonomous knowledge projects

Autonomous knowledge projects continue in the twenty-first century. A notable example is the magazine *Arena*, launched in the early 1960s by a breakaway group of Marxist intellectuals in Melbourne. It has been a forum for brilliant analyses of knowledge work, Australian society and global politics. The group organized as a cooperative, learned the printing trade and published their own books and magazines. The German magazine *Das Argument* has a similar trajectory. Indeed there is a worldwide genre of autonomous magazines that link activism, research and journalism, including the feminist *Manushi* in India (launched in 1978 and crowd-funded in pre-internet style), the feminist *Agenda* in South Africa (autonomous for twenty years, now published by Taylor & Francis) and the online *The New Inquiry* in the United States.[16]

Recently there has been a revival of Free University ideas. The Free University of New York City launched in 2012, coming out of the Occupy Wall Street movement. It is a network that organizes 'free, crowd-sourced education' in a variety of public spaces – the main model is a one-off workshop rather than a continuing course. FUNYC has produced an organizing manual, *How to Free U*, to encourage other groups. The Free University in Brisbane gives lectures and discussions in public spaces, with a notable innovation: they meet in a car park in downtown Brisbane. The overall picture of these initiatives is creative, messy, diverse, and resource-poor – progressive education, on the traditional shoestring.[17]

A lot of autonomous activism in the global North is now online, or at least networked online. It is easy to explore the websites that show this activity, some ephemeral, some lasting. Among the interesting initiatives are the US-based Undercommoning project, with a concern to connect social struggles inside and outside mainstream universities (www.undercommoning.org); in Britain, the Ragged University (www.raggeduniversity.co.uk); in Canada, the Vancouver Institute for Social Research (www.visrfreeschool.wordpress.com). There are many more.

Other adult education projects have taken the name 'university'. One of the most interesting is the University of the Third Age, U3A. This is a network of self-help education groups for older people, retired or semi-retired. It emphasizes low cost, knowledge-sharing, and local control. U3A got under way in Europe in the 1970s and now claims 3000 groups internationally.

Struggles for wider social access to education have taken many forms. Residential Folk High Schools began in Denmark in the mid-nineteenth century, offering non-credentialled, humanist courses for social groups who had no access to academic pathways. They are still running in northern and central Europe. The Folk University in Sweden is something different. This is a development of the old practice known as 'university extension', where academic staff of mainstream universities gave lectures for free, especially in the evening, to adult audiences. Departments of extramural studies were set up in many universities to organize this work.

They have declined under the market regime, of course, but some carry on: the Swedish Folk University is an alliance of five of them.[18]

Such outreach and knowledge-sharing projects may have little interest in research. But there are also popular science and popular history movements that centre on producing knowledge, whose work goes into family histories, local museums, and so forth. Some citizen-research projects have become highly organized and are practically social movements in their own right (see Box 9). These link with academic disciplines, though they are not simply a branch of university research.

9 Dig Where You Stand: citizen research

I learnt how knowledge production could be a social movement at a fascinating talk by the writer Sven Lindqvist. He described a movement in working-class communities in Sweden, supported by the unions. The idea was for workers in a particular factory or workplace to research the history of their own jobs, to understand their current situation better. That took them into the broader history of their industry and region, into changing technologies, social structures and labour relations.

Working-class people are not usually imagined as researchers; but who better? They start by knowing a lot about their own jobs, their workplaces, their co-workers and their bosses. Lindqvist's copiously illustrated book *Gräv där du står* (Dig Where You Stand) shows the wealth of materials they turn up: photographs, diaries, letter-books, maps, court proceedings, production statistics, family budgets, machinery, and of course the ruins of the earlier economy. Industrial archaeology in glorious detail![19]

(continued)

(continued)

In 2013–15 a frightening epidemic broke out in West Africa, resulting in eleven thousand deaths. In his book *Ebola: How a People's Science Helped End an Epidemic*, Paul Richards tells how local people worked out the epidemiology of the virus, and devised techniques of the body that allowed them to care for the sick and bury the dead while preventing further spread of the disease. This reminded me of the way gay communities, in the 1980s, grasped what was happening with AIDS and invented the 'safe sex' strategy that has been vital in resisting the HIV pandemic.[20]

Birdwatching is often treated as comedy – hearing the First Cuckoo of Spring, and then writing a letter to *The Times* about it, used to be a national joke in England. In fact, amateur ornithology is a large-scale data collection enterprise and a notable source of information about ecosystem changes, including effects of global warming. Amateur astronomy, too, has extensive networks of observers who teach each other. The British Astronomical Association, more than a hundred years old, has a 'BAA Observing Community' with impressive levels of expertise. In other countries too, amateurs work with professionals in trawling though masses of automated observations looking for the light signature of an exoplanet orbiting a distant star – and new planets have been found this way.[21]

Local communities may also do social research on contemporary problems. Confronting the 'fragmented, informal, invisible work' that many women do, the Spanish group *Precarias a la deriva* launched urban research with a method they call 'drifting', exploring the settings of each others' daily lives and trying to define a relevant politics. From Australia, Yoland Wadsworth's

Do It Yourself Social Research is a best-selling handbook for participatory action research, precise in methodology, humorous and accessible in style. Its successive editions have connected an international network of activists, NGOs and academics, who share the approach pioneered by the great Colombian sociologist Orlando Fals Borda.[22]

The pressures of the market turn described in Chapter 6 have provoked student protest, industrial unrest and union action. As well as autonomous projects, they have triggered reform initiatives inside established universities (Box 10).

10 Within the walls

A campaign by some academic staff contests the pressure for speed-up, the mad demand to compress teaching and produce ever more publications in ever-shorter times. They promote Slow Scholarship, taking inspiration from the 'slow food' campaign against industrialized fast food. In a charming book called *The Slow Professor*, the Canadian scholars Maggie Berg and Barbara Seeber give simple practical suggestions such as walking to the library, not just accessing it online (assuming there is a good library, of course).[23]

Better known is the Open Access movement. Some research funders insist that the research they finance has to be published without paywalls. The open access principle has gained traction in Latin America: most journals in the region are accessible to anyone, free of charge. CODESRIA, the Council for the Development

(continued)

(continued)

of Social Science Research in Africa, also publishes its journals on this basis. In the global North, new free-access journals have been set up. The most famous is *PLOS One*, the initials standing for Public Library Of Science. This is not free of charge to the writers.[24]

The idea of open access was taken up by the Russian neuroscientist Alexandra Elbakyan, who did something bold. She set up a website called *Sci-Hub*, which gives free access to millions of research papers. (Try her website!) The publishing corporation Elsevier is taking her to court, charging this is piracy. Elbakyan's response is that these publishers are breaking Article 27 of the Universal Declaration of Human Rights. In another famous case, the US activist Aaron Swartz used a computer at MIT to put a large volume of scientific papers from JSTOR into the public domain. He was pursued by government prosecutors for this action, charged with multiple crimes, and in despair killed himself.[25]

In 2001 MIT began to put its own course documents online, and ten years later partnered with Harvard University to set up the widely used platform *edX*. This is a mixture of university extension and commercialization. It is open-source, but claims to connect learners with 'the world's best universities', and includes as partners Microsoft and the World Bank.[26]

Much grittier projects arose at the same time, such as the Freedom University Georgia in the United States. In the early 2000s the deepening racism of Republican Party politics led officials in Georgia to exclude 'undocumented' (immigrant) students from state universities. In 2011 some academics at the University of Georgia launched voluntary courses to support these students. This work has grown into an immigrant-rights activist centre and a larger teaching programme, qualifying students for university entrance in other parts of the country.[27]

Universities have not been pacified. Contestation and invention continue today, with persistent links to liberatory social struggles beyond the universities.

Struggle and joy: lessons of experience

All these projects have faced problems about resources. Visva-Bharati ran into a funding crisis; the shoestring finances of Free Universities frayed; indigenous communities don't have many billionaires. If alternative universities do not have government backing or a revenue stream from fees, they are likely to remain small and fragile. In particular, they find it hard to support a workforce adequate to their hopes. Most university reform agendas I have seen, except for union proposals, have little to say about workforce issues. Some say *nothing* about the operations staff, as if a reformed university could float in the air, operated only by academics.

A common consequence of thin resources is burnout. Movement-based projects like the Free Universities and autonomous magazines, relying on intense commitment and voluntary labour from a bunch of activists, easily became unsustainable. The greenfields universities called out tremendous commitment from their staff in early years, but found it hard to keep the fire burning with the same intensity. Yet some radical knowledge projects sustained themselves for decades and even longer. There is currently a remarkable regeneration of indigenous knowledge. The social ferment about knowledge continues, even when particular projects do not.

In the front garden of the Free University in Sydney stood a large hand-painted sign saying 'Free U – All Welcome'. The idea of open participation stands in stark opposition to the privilege machines of the official university world. It is a driving force in many of the reform projects just discussed. As the SEEK programme at City College of New York showed, 'All Welcome' demands active recruitment and changes to curriculum. It means criticizing cultural exclusions, finding new teaching materials, and re-thinking writing, tests and quizzes, i.e. much of the everyday apparatus of academic work.

'All Welcome' also sharpens the issue of resources. To be genuinely inclusive means operating on a societal scale and prioritizing social justice. Without a way to do that, new knowledge projects are likely to become new preserves of privilege. Many citizen-science projects, for instance, depend on volunteers who have leisure, and enough spare money to buy equipment like telescopes. A crucial limit on many radical projects was that they did not attempt professional education. This may have been on principle – rejecting closure and privilege – but it seriously limited the economic contribution that alternative universities could make.

The solution to resource problems for some projects – the postwar greenfields universities, the recent Pink Tide initiatives, and the postcolonial al-Azhar – was investment by the state. This gave scale, permanence, and credibility. It also brought vulnerability to the politics of state power. The greenfields universities were later exposed to the market agenda's slashing of public investment. In 2016 the Workers Party government in Brazil was thrown out in a constitutional coup. For other alternative projects, the state was always an enemy. The Flying University was under police pressure; the Midpeninsula Free University was, the archives revealed later, under heavy FBI surveillance; Freedom University Georgia is under attack now. Shariati's alternative university was choked off by the Shah's security police; Mexican students were shot down. Who sups with the devil, needs a long spoon. If the state is a solution to the problem of resources, it is a dangerous solution.

Many of the projects have tapped sources outside the mainstream knowledge economy: indigenous knowledges, Islamic sciences, Asian civilizations, local knowledges, the head trips of the counter-culture, and more. This has been very important in expanding the picture of knowledge. But because the established economy of knowledge has power and money, 'alternative' usually means 'embattled'. It is easy for embattled projects to become defensive, even dogmatic.

What impresses me most, taking these reform movements and alternative university projects together, is their joy, creativity and energy. Some initiatives are short-lived, some run into fierce opposition, some get taken over; it is a story of struggle, not easy achievement. But by heaven, they keep coming!

Joy is a word not often spoken about today's market-oriented universities. But there should be joy in learning, in making knowledge, in solving problems, in sharing, in making new things possible. Most reform projects would have died very quickly without this joy. That so many projects have grown is a sign of the imagination and creativity that can be found among a multitude of participants.

It is also a sign of unmet needs. Many of the new projects challenged the exclusions perpetrated by privilege machines. Some addressed dogmatism and closure in the research-based knowledge formation. Some found a distinctive local basis, such as indigenous knowledge, or the local knowledge in teaching and research that serves the needs of migrants, racialized minorities and urban working classes.

There is no master source of change, and no ideal solution to all the problems. Differences between these projects are significant and not always reconcilable. I doubt that Visva-Bharati could ever combine with al-Azhar, nor an Andean *cosmovisión* with the British Astronomical Association's Observing Community. In fact the sheer variety of viable knowledge projects is one of their most important lessons. The aristocratic universities of Europe and the United States *cannot* provide the ideal for all universities, whatever the league tables say. We have to accept that there are multiple pathways into the future for universities.

Multiplicity poses risks. Movements for university reform are seriously fragmented at present, and that has given advantage to the corporate agenda. But there is rich experience in connecting across differences. Both Visva-Bharati and al-Azhar have negotiated relations between knowledge formations within their own walls. Indigenous universities deal with the research-based knowledge formation as well as ancestral knowledge. There are increasing numbers of South/South connections, in research fields from climate to human sexuality. We can draw on powerful intellectual work based on cross-fertilizations: Frantz Fanon, connecting psychiatry with anti-colonial struggle; Ali Shariati, connecting Shiite theology with European radical sociology; Sandra Harding, connecting feminist epistemology with postcolonial thought.[28]

Reform projects have also taught important lessons about organization. They have shown, in quite practical ways, that universities do not need god-professors or gold-plated managers. Teaching, research and decision-making can all be done in democratic ways. Engagement pedagogies are part of a great tradition in education that highlights the capacities of the learner and the power of collective learning. They do not make teaching irrelevant: *acompañamiento* is an active, highly skilled role. Many projects have developed self-managed research groups and independent publications. Some mainstream universities have learned to cooperate with citizen science, or respond to local research needs.[29]

Alternative universities have used general meetings and elections to manage their affairs. They build on a very long tradition of self-management and representative bodies within universities. In the past, operations staff have often been excluded from decision-making, but some reform projects have shown them taking the initiative. The Open University's creative work in distance education, led by new groups of technical staff, is a case in point.[30]

The real-life experiences of alternative universities and reform projects have brought out extraordinary possibilities in university work, while confronting some of its major problems. In the final chapter I try to bring this experience to bear on future pathways, and the basic idea of a good university.

Chapter 8

The good university

The good university already exists – in many fragments. In this chapter I ask how the fragments might come together.

The choice of futures

In earlier chapters I traced the making of a worldwide university system. In the last few decades enrolment has expanded spectacularly, while the institutions have been transformed by the market agenda and managerialism. The old centre/periphery relation has become a steep global hierarchy of university-firms, with wealth and prestige concentrated where they are least needed.

In the mirror of the market we can see a possible future for this system. In this future all universities become proper firms, owned by investors and managers. All operations work is outsourced, and all of the teachers are sessional. Staff are appointed by managers. Curricula are trimmed back to fee-earning vocational programmes. Teaching is done online by the cheapest labour available in global markets, under automated surveillance. The most profitable universities have no campuses at all, just brands, managers, and online systems. National hierarchies of university-firms exist, under a global hierarchy of English-language universities. Only those at the top conduct research. All the research they do depends on military or corporate funding.

That is a fantasy – but uncomfortably close to what crystal-ball-gazers at management consultancy firms are already projecting as the future for universities.[1] Going farther and faster down the corporate track is supported by a powerful alliance of university managers, the finance and publishing industries, the wider corporate elite, state officials (including international agencies like OECD and World Bank), and powerful politicians in all major states.

This is a formidable line-up. In the ordinary course of events one would not expect to make much headway against them. But unexpected things have been happening. We have seen growing anger among university workers in the face of insecurity, stress and wage stagnation. Their discontent is shown in surveys, in the chorus of criticism since the 1990s, and in the greatly increased number of strikes, boycotts and bans in recent years. Also unexpected, in a period of growth, is the scale of community anger about unequal access. Protests against privilege machines range from the 'Fees Must Fall' movement in South Africa to Dalit student protests in India. Because so much of the recent expansion has been funded by fees, in the background looms the wicked problem of massive and increasing student debt.

Unexpected, too, is the scale of challenges to natural science and concepts of truth. These range from climate change denialism and fundamentalist anti-evolutionism, to the flood of 'alternative facts' (as one Trump aide called them) in social media and official statements. They show a troubling erosion of legitimacy for the knowledge formation on which universities depend.

It has become obvious that the market regime is far from a smoothly functioning machine. Deregulation and tax cuts allowed the rich to grab short-term gains at the cost of long-term stability. Corporate capital has been moving offshore, into global finance markets that now outweigh most national economies. Structural unemployment and steeper inequalities have followed. Whole sectors have been wiped out: there are now rust belts in the global South as well as in the North. Transnational corporations operate practically free of democratic controls. Market-driven development is causing worldwide destruction of forests, ocean habitats and biological diversity, and driving the climate crisis. Self-sustaining rural communities around the global South are in steep decline, with mass migration into cities and the rise of monoculture and GM crops.

It is not really surprising that mass insecurity, resentment and fear are prominent in politics today. Under these pressures, some oligarchs have already abandoned elements of the neoliberal model, notably free trade and separation of powers. We have reached a time when other social models again look possible. Unfortunately a revived authoritarianism is one of them.

Our historical moment holds other possibilities. There are movements for economic justice, for gender and racial equality, and for defence of the environment, worldwide. The global economy is incredibly productive and could eliminate world poverty now. Some countries still maintain a welfare state or an inclusive development agenda. Despite the exploitation, violence and horror in our world, there is cultural ferment too, with new artistic movements, new media and new syntheses of ideas.

Universities embody some of these alternatives. University research continues to produce disturbing and important knowledge, not least about environmental crisis. Many university workers still believe in public service more than profit. Many students still arrive with a thirst for new ideas, not just job tickets. In the wider society, despite 'post-truth' politics, there is a continuing demand for knowledge, and respect for the people who produce and teach it.

There are better futures that we can choose for universities – by *collective* choice, not the individual decision of a market consumer. This will require mobilizing social resources on a large scale. But in what direction?

Criteria for a good university …

In the practices of university staff and students everywhere, and in the debates and experiments discussed in this book, there are abundant ideas about good education, good research, and good ways of running universities. They do not offer alternative ranking scales; they do speak to the real issues we are facing.

The essential starting-point is the fact, which I have hammered unmercifully through this book, that universities are real, working organizations, with real workforces, real environments, and real effects. Their research, their teaching and their operations are a weave of collective labour. To speak of a good university is to think about this collective activity and its possible futures. Gathering the discussions from earlier chapters, I propose that a good university is democratic, engaged, truthful, creative, and sustainable.

Democratic means that the organization operates in a democratic way, and serves democratic purposes for its society. A good university is an industrial democracy, with equality in wages and conditions, shared decision-making and shared responsibility. The multiple, interlocking labour processes of research and higher education need constant coordination. Who can do that better than the people who know them best, who actually do the work? In a good university all the workforce are managers. We know lots of ways to run organizations more democratically, this is not a deep secret. Universities have experience with them. The key point is that democratic practices become routine, not exceptional. A good university develops a democratic culture.

This applies in the university's relations with its society. Reproducing privileged elites is not a legitimate use of social resources. In both teaching and research a good university follows principles of social justice, giving priority to the *least* advantaged social groups. Research can support sustainable agriculture, good nutrition, and effective schools in disadvantaged areas. Social justice is also core business for the teaching programme, both in democratizing access, and pursuing curricular justice in the courses.

A good university is a good place to work, for *all* its workforce. It has job security and workforce stability. It fosters staff skills and knowledge. It values operations staff as highly as it values academics. Running a university involves a great quantity of administrative, technical and manual work; *every* function of a university depends on the work of operations staff. A university with high ambitions depends even more on their creativity and commitment.

Engaged means being fully present for the society that supports the university. A good university's research agendas respond to social needs for knowledge, at local and global scale. Local needs inform agricultural or fisheries research, health, education and social science, all giving scope for working with local communities and citizen science. On the wider scale, a good university is not shy about addressing questions of war and peace, of global justice, of environment and the fate of the planet.

The curriculum in a good university engages with difficult, resonant questions where the answers are not known. It invites students to a strenuous learning project, not an easy one. That applies in professional programmes as much as in arts, humanities or pure sciences. In professional education, as well as the techniques of the trade, a good university offers exploration of the techniques' foundations, debate about their justifications, and encounters with research-based knowledge around them.

Good teaching means being fully present for the students, engaging with their actual needs and enabling their next moves in learning. The pedagogy of engagement is demanding for teachers in time and emotion as well as technical knowledge.

They must get to know specific groups of students, work with them, think about the resources and skills they need, and support them through a sustained learning process. Therefore a good university needs a secure teaching workforce and does most of its educational work face to face.

Truthful concerns the detail of university operations as well as the way the university presents itself to the world. In the research-based knowledge formation, truth is not defined by a single state of knowledge, but is a property of the practices through which knowledge is developed. A good university does research in a truthful way. It works positively towards completeness of evidence, powerful analysis, consistency of argument and systematic critique. It supports the expansion of research-based knowledge in practical ways such as educating the citizen-science workforce.

Teaching in the presence of research-based knowledge has the same criterion of truthful practice. We are not free to teach lies or distortions. A curriculum always selects, not to suppress knowledge, rather to open pathways and enable critique. In a good university, teaching will emphasize how knowledge is produced and archived, helping students test claims, challenge received knowledge, and conduct their own investigations.

It is a university's job to serve its society, not to agree with it. Where there are uncomfortable findings, it is the university's job to declare them. Intellectual labour involves a constant flow of questioning and critique. That is a crucial resource for societies facing difficulty and change, feeling their way into unknown futures. A good university, inevitably, is a bearer of oppositional ideas, an obstacle to privilege.

Creative has a particular meaning for universities: it relates to the dynamism of knowledge formations and educational processes. Creativity in research means expanding the archive, devising new forms of encounter with materials, imaginative patterning, and linking different knowledge formations. What Jane Kenway and Johanna Fahey call 'the research imagination' grows out of conditions that support adventurous work. Academic freedom is only part of this. Just as important are workforce security, funding for the full labour process of research, and an organizational culture that trusts staff to use time and resources well.[2]

A good university foregrounds student agency in learning. Students do creative work when they study: it is they, not the teachers, who build the new intellectual structures in their own minds. This work needs organizational support. Much of it comes from operations staff in libraries, offices, laboratories and workshops, so a good university provides ways for them to work together with students. Since solutions are not known in advance, a good university supports variety and invention in teaching. It has space for wildness in classrooms, mad professors, and educational risk-taking – knowing that only some of them will succeed.

Sustainable means the capacity to flourish as an organization over the long run. A university is not a pop-up shop: its work needs time to unfold. That needs a steady source of income, which most alternative-university projects have struggled to find. It needs resilience in the face of disruption, change and political pressure.

Sustainability concerns both the university's organizational life and its relation with the knowledge economy. A good university's employment conditions support its workers, both operations and academic staff, over the long run. As a healthy workplace, a good university limits stress on staff, as well as limiting industrial accidents. It creates conditions for the renewal of the workforce from one generation to another. On a larger scale, it sustains the knowledge economy as a whole. A good university freely circulates information, ideas and techniques, and acts steadily to build a knowledge commons in the world at large.

Being sustainable means working within resource limits, and this connects with the idea of a democratic culture. A good university does not build palaces for itself. It lives at the level of its society as a whole. This is a serious matter. It goes to the credibility of the institution, the responsible use of social resources, and respect for what actually matters in university life. A good university will have a modest demeanour in the world. When it needs to teach in a shack, it will teach in a shack.

... and a good university system

A major theme emerging through this book is that to make good universities, we need good university systems. None of the criteria just mentioned can be realized in isolation. Some issues can only be approached on a national or international scale.

In everyday practice, universities constantly share with each other. They read each others' publications and support the same scientific organizations. They hire each others' graduates, and hire each others' staff for senior positions. They provide each other with higher degree students, research colleagues, curricula, technologies and models of practice. They are jointly the targets of funding cuts, media abuse, and other signs of esteem. For public policy it is the university system that matters, much more than the individual university.

One criterion for a good university system, therefore, can be stated very simply. A good university system is cooperative rather than antagonistic and competitive. Whatever the level of resources, the work will be most effective – and efficient – if universities consistently give each other respect and support. Only a system organized for cooperation will allow specialization, division of labour, regional and institutional diversity, and sharing of facilities, without institutions having to fear they will lose status or money.

The great issues about university funding are the source, and the distribution. I will be brief about the source. State funding through a redistributive tax system is the only currently available method that is compatible with democratic purposes for a university system. All young people should have the right to go to university, or to technical college or non-vocational further education, or later in life return to education; and none of these pathways should be distorted by economic inequalities. For students, there should be a solid advanced-education guarantee; and only public funding will provide that.

Democratizing access is a major issue in all university systems, and has implications for the institutions. A universal guarantee would become a farce if a privileged minority of universities could cream off resources and prestige. A good university system is marked by equality among universities. This is not a fantastic dream. A number of countries had a high level of economic equality among universities a generation ago – in Australia, for instance, every academic worker was on the common national wage scale – and it was often the newer and less-known universities that were the most exciting.

No issue about universities is more important, or more difficult, than the global economy of knowledge. Individual universities can work on global relations at any time, but the basic issues are beyond any one university's means. Inequality between university systems is enmeshed with Northern hegemony in the economy of knowledge, and the exclusion of other knowledge formations. There is a struggle about scientific recognition in Latin America right now, with the SciELO database intended to highlight local publications. There is a struggle globally to recognize and value local knowledges, indigenous knowledges and alternative universalisms. Rabindranath Tagore was right: a good university will be a meeting-place of cultures. But Tagore could not find a sustainable way to do it with just one institution.

In my view, the key to more productive connections is the way different knowledge formations undertake the *growth* of knowledge. All of them do; it is a complete mistake to think of indigenous or Islamic or Ayurvedic knowledge as static.

New learning occurs at the point of growth, and it is in the broadening and revision of knowledge archives that other formations most readily play a fertilizing role. In this terrain, the criterion of a good university system is its deep diversity, engaging with a whole ecology of knowledge formations, not a monoculture.

Global hegemony grew out of imperial power. We would like to think of the modern university world as autonomous, but influence still depends on where the money is. The income of universities in the rich countries of the global North is not just double that of universities in most of the global South; it is around ten times more. Material poverty affects the migration of students and staff, participation in international conferences, labour processes inside universities, and research. Since the 1950s much research around the global South has been funded by international aid, which comes with donor influence and narrow intellectual purposes; experience shows this is hard to change.[3]

Regional cooperation is one way of building up research resources and challenging hegemony. South/South cooperation is certainly on the agenda now, and there is good experience in organizations such as CODESRIA and CLACSO. Reliable funding is harder to achieve: in 2017 the South African government, for one, announced sharp cuts to its broad-based research funding scheme. There is not yet any policy consensus about global relations in the university world. But we can state a final criterion for a good university system: it will be redistributive on a world scale.

Manifestos and visions

How do we move from definitions and criteria to agendas of change? Proposals for the future have been surfacing in a suddenly-popular genre: the university manifesto. I would like to introduce four (see box).

The charming 'Slow university: a manifesto' was issued in 2006 by Brian Treanor, a philosopher at Loyola Marymount University in the United States. Treanor was upset at the growing corporatization of his university and its demand for speed-ups. So he posted on his office door an announcement of 'slow hours' (12.00 to 1.00 on Mondays, Wednesdays and Fridays, 11.00 to 12.00 on Tuesdays and Thursdays, and all day Sundays) during which he would answer no emails, do no teaching and write no papers for publication. What he would do in those hours was talk to people, and think. Two years later he recorded ruefully that just one colleague had followed his example.[4]

In 2015 three Australian feminists, Jane Kenway, Rebecca Boden and Johanna Fahey, published 'Seeking the necessary "resources of hope" in the neoliberal university'. They note the danger of despair as the managerial juggernaut rolls on and the university becomes a 'paranoid, defensive institution' that ignores all critique. So they set out to find actions and spaces that do give hope. They found many: a cooperative university in Spain, student activism in Australia, cross-cultural teaching in Hong Kong, defiant research imagination, industrial struggles, and more. Their account gives full weight to the emotional dimension of research, teaching and organizational life. And it is beautifully written.[5]

In the fierce debates triggered by the 'Rhodes Must Fall' movement in South Africa, the Cameroonian historian, critic and philosopher Achille Mbembe gave public lectures which he wrote up in 2016 as 'Decolonizing the university: new directions'. Mbembe supports the campaign to take racist memorials out of the university. But he argues that decolonization is not achieved by nationalism, that it involves 'profoundly intellectual' questions.

Recalling Frantz Fanon and Ngũgĩ wa Thiong'o, Mbembe argues for taking a wider, in fact global, perspective. On the global scale, however, universities are being transformed with stunning speed into service centres for transnational capital, creating a workforce for a commodified, financialized world. University research is complicit in the destruction of the natural world and in the emergence of a new techno-racism. The task of decolonizing universities is therefore linked to our capacity to re-think the global economy and human mutuality.[6]

In 2013 Willem Halffman and Hans Radder published in the Dutch journal *Krisis* 'The academic manifesto: from an occupied to a public university'. An English translation appeared two years later. Halffman and Radder make a familiar critique of market-oriented managers, whom they regard as an occupying force ('The Wolf', in contrast with academics as the sheep). Their alternative is also familiar: 'a public university aimed at the common good'. What is unusual is their detail about how to launch the change. They offer 20 provocative first moves: valuing the operations staff, banning mergers and marketing, placing limits on surveillance and control systems, sharing teaching across the academic staff, and so on. Since The Wolf is impervious to argument, they also propose actions to force change: working-to-rule, strikes and occupations, parliamentary pressure, creating contra-indicators of the state of universities, and more. It is an invigorating text.[7]

Manifestos are inspirations, but are not working models. To launch changes we need to think about specifics, and it helps to have examples. A touch of science fiction may help, and science-fiction writers have produced some very interesting visions of researchers and teachers. Among the classics are Stanislaw Lem's intimate picture of a research unit struggling with incomprehensible experience, in his famous novel *Solaris*; and Ursula Le Guin's physicist, from the working anarchist society in her novel *The Dispossessed*, grappling with the problems of social change.[8]

In this spirit let us step into the time machine and visit three possible institutions, 10, 50, and 200 years into the future. Since I am the founder of these universities, I get to choose their names. I will honour an imaginative educator from Java, a pathbreaking Australian prehistorian, a wonderful Chilean poet and a Danish pioneer of quantum physics.

10 years: Kartini Community University[9]

Kartini Community University (KCU) is a relatively new, general-purpose public university in a provincial capital in a postcolonial country. It is funded partly by regional government, partly by central government. It is all on one campus, apart from some research stations and community teaching centres. KCU has generous central spaces for eating, discussion, services, studios, clubs and performances. It also has quiet spaces for thinking, under banyan and eucalyptus trees. The buildings use materials and forms familiar in the neighbourhood, the budget does not allow fashionable architects or costly materials. But they are designed for interactive teaching, and close working relations between operations and academic staff.

The students who come to KCU are mostly locals, midlife as well as straight from school. Kartini was a pioneer of women's education under Dutch rule in the colonized East Indies, and KCU makes a serious attempt at inclusiveness in terms of gender, class background, and ethnicity. The staff are mostly full-time; they have modest salaries compared with the metropole but they have job security and support for professional learning. That makes for a stable workforce who build up institutional know-how and professional skills, and are able to coordinate the labour process from below. Operations staff and academic staff are on the same pay scale, and the Gini index is being reduced year by year.

A central issue for KCU is combining organizational democracy with relevance, especially to its immediate community. KCU offers a weave of general and professional courses, as the community expects and needs. The professional courses in engineering, agriculture, health and education meet basic requirements for accreditation, but also emphasize the linking of professional knowledge with research-based knowledge, with critical thought generally, and with social need specifically. KCU teachers have a portfolio of engagement pedagogies, and students are widely involved in course design. The programmes are designed as the bases for life-long learning – which is also seen as a community need.

The courses reflect KCU's postcolonial situation and engagement across cultures. Local knowledge and Islamic sciences are recognized and the curriculum provides for all students to engage with them. Exploring relationships between knowledge formations is widely recognized as a specialty of KCU researchers. Accordingly KCU needs multiple language capacities, including the languages in the community it serves.

The research pursued is extremely varied, as a matter of policy – KCU's emphasis is on breadth. The university supplies modest basic funding to *all* its research-trained staff who have projects to pursue. In fields where research has to be done on a larger scale, only a few projects can be funded and tough choices have to be made. For this reason KCU conducts a yearly scan of emerging fields of research *and* local knowledge needs. All departments participate in this, whether they like it or not, and younger staff and graduate students – who do most of the scanning! – have a voice in research policy.

Most decision-making at KCU is done by the staff and students concerned with the process in question. Central decision-making such as budgeting is done by elected bodies, and central office-holders are responsible to those bodies. Elected community members sit on the main university council, and on the bodies that do long-term planning of the courses that the university will offer.

KCU offers its region direct access to higher education, reflected in its funding. It offers its community a variety of venues and events; research addressing local problems; and support for schools, arts and citizen science. At the same time KCU is part of a national system and a worldwide economy of knowledge. It supports open access initiatives, and tries to fund conference and study travel for junior staff. So far as one university can, it supports the sharing of knowledge resources on a world scale.

50 years: The Childe Institute of World Climate Archaeology

Vere Gordon Childe, a founder of scientific prehistory, was a radical socialist – one reason he was obliged to leave Australia and make a university career in the metropole. As a prehistorian he was a great synthesizer with a world perspective on the development of human societies. Since his time, climatology has developed greatly and its links with archaeology are well recognized. Among other things, this connection underpins the concept of the 'anthropocene' era.

I assume this field will grow on a world scale over the next 50 years, with profound implications for the social sciences. World climate archaeology involves a synthesis across very large but fragmentary databases, both human and natural; multiple languages; dispersed fieldwork; several physical sciences and advanced computing; and complex issues in social science and epistemology. It is not a project that an institution like KCU could afford. Specialized centres will be needed. Can they be reconciled with a democratic agenda for universities?

The Childe Institute tries to reconcile them by building on familiar practices that link many universities in shared projects. The Institute does not 'belong' to a single university; it has modest premises near a city that has several universities of its own. Its personnel are mainly academic and operations staff on five-year secondments from contributing universities on all continents, and graduate students from all over.

The researchers use advances in information science to connect with stored data and current projects in the home countries, to translate texts extensively, and to access remote computing power. The Institute is supported by crowd-funding from participating universities plus redistributive funding from development agencies. Its decision-making bodies are elected from current staff, current students, and the contributing universities.

In an inclusive, global university system, encounters across disciplines and knowledge formations occur on a much larger scale. Universities are epistemologically much busier, and philosophers have jobs again! Some of them work at the Childe Institute, where research teams roam among translations and hybridizations as well as quantitative models, plodding across cultural bridges and panting up ladders between meta-levels.

Attempting ambitious syntheses, and thinking about the human meanings of climate change, mean that researchers face the question of incompatibility between knowledge formations. Early climate modelling used mathematical abstractions of a highly generalized kind. But place-based indigenous knowledges reference specific landscapes – hills, waterholes, tracks, plant communities, seasons – and particular social groups in those landscapes. Learning across such differences requires ethical thinking, respectful interaction, and decolonization of knowledge. That is the terrain on which the Childe Institute tries to work.

200 years: The Mistral-Bohr waystation of University-b

If humans survive the next two centuries, we should be living in societies where advanced knowledge is not just a universal right but a universal reality. The information society as realized today by Microsoft, Google and Apple is mainly a society of knowledge consumers. But university teaching and learning develop autonomous capacities to evaluate and construct knowledge. The citizen-researcher movements, as well as engaged pedagogies, point towards a society of knowledge *producers*.

Moving towards a society of knowledge producers will re-shape the experience of knowledge. If it is not embedded in a struggle for advantage, then learning can become more a matter of joy, integrating craft and art. Producing and broadcasting knowledge will not be sharply separated from other forms of production and circulation. Making, using and enjoying knowledge will be a regular part of living well. In Andean countries the idea of *buen vivir* has been proposed to replace the mechanistic model of economic development. The idea does not reject material well-being, but values equally the quality of social relations and the integrity of the natural environment.

University work could be transformed by being dispersed, with knowledge production as a thread woven through many social settings and cultural practices. The powers of universities, as educators and makers of culture, would be realized through a very different organizational geometry. But change in that direction would risk fragmentation and loss of critique. To counter this, universities, rather than being distinct containers of knowledge, might become waystations to which large numbers of people return for varying periods of intense knowledge work and reconsideration.

If we call the current container format *university-a*, we could call this format of thread-and-waystation *university-b*. I propose a waystation named Mistral-Bohr for the drama of arts and sciences: Gabriela Mistral who wrote poetry across boundaries of place, culture and nature; Niels Bohr who saw the quantum logic of the atom and tried, too late, to stop the atomic arms race. *University-b* needs Mistral-Bohr because when knowledge has moved beyond familiar forms, the process creates new problems of boundaries, uses, and threats.

I cannot picture my waystation concretely, as architecture two centuries ahead may not be using concrete. But I am sure Mistral-Bohr will be an actual place, not a virtual site. Personal talk, and practices of meditation, will be vital for a waystation. It will be a place for slowing down (the 'slow professor' has a participatory future here), for unfamiliar meetings, for withdrawal and reflection, as well as for intense bouts of new learning.

Archives and broadcasting will take new forms, but encounter, patterning and critique will still be needed. The participants will make new interweavings of science and art, syntheses far beyond the computer art and multimedia that we know today. I hope they still have the kind of experience Mistral described in the first stanza of a sequence of poems about time:

> Hincho mi corazón para que entre
> como cascada ardiente el Universo.
> El nuevo día llega y su llegada
> me deja sin aliento.
> Canto como la gruta que es colmada
> canto mi día nuevo.[10]
>
> I open my heart so the universe
> can enter like a burning cascade.
> The new day comes and its coming
> leaves me breathless.
> I sing like a brimful valley,
> I sing my new day.

Now take a deep breath, step out of the time machine, and be welcomed back to the vale of tears we live in today.

Taking action

We live in interesting times. One purpose of this book is to show what these times mean for universities: a mature research-based knowledge formation, a mass teaching project, Northern hegemony in the economy of knowledge, global inequalities, powerful machineries of privilege, an ascendant market agenda, managerial takeovers, diffuse resistance, and a rich history of alternatives. University systems have expanded greatly, and become more troubled, more openly sites of exploitation, deception and conflict.

We have created a worldwide intellectual workforce, on a scale never seen before. The cooperative labour of this workforce has built mass higher education, and research so abundant and varied that it is almost impossible to map. A tremendous resource has been created.

This resource is social as well as technical. I started with boring chapters about research and teaching to show the democracy lurking in the basic work of universities. Cooperation and self-management can be found in research, in teaching and learning, in offices and workshops – in all the work that creates the university day by day. Perhaps the fizz is fizziest in the experiments discussed in Chapter 7, but it can be heard, quietly, in every university.

There is a widespread humanism among university workers, and a widespread belief in universities as a public good. The commitment to truth has been battered by the market turn, but remains fundamental to research and teaching. Universities are, in principle, open to more inclusive knowledge projects, as shown by Visva-Bharati, Al-Azhar, Te Whare Wananga o Awanuiarangi, and others. Immense prospects are opened up by the multiplication of researchable zones, the creativity of teachers, the linking of disciplines and the interweaving of knowledge formations.

Only a fraction of this potential has yet been realized. Established power structures steer university work into narrow channels and trap its potential. For good universities to grow and flourish, these power structures have to be challenged. We need to end Northern hegemony, Southern dependency, and the marginalization of alternative knowledge formations. We need to break down race, class and caste exclusions, patriarchal privilege, and the links between elite universities and corporate power. Within universities, we need to end managerial control, the selling of access, the commercialization of knowledge, and the culture of lying.

A big ask? Certainly. Strap in for a rough ride! At the start of this chapter I sketched a possible future of more private universities, bloodier competition, deeper inequality and grimmer alienation. The groups pushing us towards that future make a powerful alliance, but not all-powerful. They are being challenged, and some trends are already slipping out of their grasp. Other futures are possible. In practical terms, who might support a more democratic future for universities?

Many university workers will. Very large numbers are now affected by low pay and insecurity, loss of control over one's own work, rising pressure for output, and rising stress and anxiety. The unions that represent university workers speak to these issues, and will be central in strategies of change. Unions face dilemmas: divisions among staff, and the need to address immediate grievances and bargaining. Yet they are the key source of long-term thinking about the sector.

Students and their families may also support change, especially those outside the charmed circles of privilege. As enrolments have expanded and costs have been shifted onto students' families, the financial pressures have got heavier. In situations of mass poverty, raising cash and forgoing income are extremely difficult. Increasing numbers of graduates move into adult life with a heavy debt burden. Students arrive on campus with hope, and deserve better than the routine experience they mostly find. The many students who are 'first in family' need changes in curriculum and pedagogy, and bring cultural resources into the university, though these often go unrecognized.[11]

And remember the alumnae! Not as managerial universities see them – cash cows waiting to be milked – but as active participants in the economy of knowledge. University graduates become an intellectual workforce spread through the professions, the arts, the media, the health sector, the schools and the corporate world. They have an interest in keeping contact with organized knowledge. Privatized universities and paywalls are not in their interest; flourishing universities engaged in public service outreach are. (This is the basis for my sketch of *university-b*.)

There are wider groups, too, with an interest in good universities. Local communities gain from research with regional applications, higher education suited to their young people, relevant curricula, and university outreach such as engagement with local schools. (This is the basis for my sketch of Kartini Community University.) The state normally serves ruling classes, but also has long-term needs for legitimacy and cannot entirely ignore the public interest. Many public servants still have an ethic of public service: good bureaucrats exist! State agencies may go in conflicting directions – contrast Britain and Germany on university fees. Halffman and Radder's *Academic Manifesto* quite rightly includes the state as a site of action for democratic change in universities.

Putting these together, there is formidable *potential* support for good public universities working in the public interest. We can make a collective choice for such a future. To make that choice effective, however, requires more than a line-up of interest groups. It needs working alliances that can generate political strength, connection with wider social movements. and principles and agendas that unite different social forces and capture the initiative in the public arena.

The most powerful of these principles is simply to recognize the modern university as a shared social resource, a collective asset. I used this principle when defining criteria for a good university. Universities have been created by the labour of many thousands of people over many generations. Most universities have been founded and funded by governments, and even those set up privately have been given land, tax concessions, grants and contracts. All operate within a large economy of knowledge in which they are supported by the other universities of the world. To turn them into private assets is basically a crime: theft from the public. The university as an institution is not owned by anyone except society as a whole, and its benefits belong to society as a whole.

There is a lot of support for the idea of a right to higher education. This concept has been around since the 1950s, and is embedded in UN documents. It is most often phrased as an individual right, but it need not be. Education policy has often recognized the exclusion or under-representation of whole social groups. What regional universities need from their governments, more than equity targets, is an institutional funding guarantee. This allows them to plan for access by the different groups living in the region, and make the long-term changes in curriculum and pedagogy that real inclusiveness demands.[12]

Basic to any future beyond the dog-eat-dog market is the principle that universities meet collective needs. Professional degrees are the bread-and-butter of university teaching because there is a social need, not just a market demand, for a range of professions. Most university research addresses the collective need for the advancement of knowledge rather than short-term private payoffs. (This is the basis for my sketch of the Childe Institute.) Societies facing turbulent and uncertain futures need the critique, imagination and dependable knowledge that a strong university system provides – whether the issue is environmental sanity, social justice, public health or liveable cities.[13]

We realize such principles most effectively by building from below: doing it here and now, with whatever resources are at hand. There is a multitude of examples. Some start small, like Jen Bagelman's unit on campus food. Some start large, like Women's Studies which involved critique of the whole academic culture. Some are autonomous, like Visva-Bharati or the Free Universities. Some are embedded in existing institutions, like the Open Access movement. There are liberated zones, imaginative curricula, research in alliance with local communities ...

We need more of them, thousands of them, a mighty torrent ... Well, I shouldn't get carried away. But I do emphasize that building from below is both part of a strategy of change, and part of what a good university *is*. Prefigurative action, to use the old term. It's exhilarating, too.[14]

But we also need to build from above. I have emphasized the importance of university systems, not just individual universities. A democratic agenda has to work at this level too, and reach social compacts about the tasks of universities and their long-term funding. That is not out of the question: there have been such compacts in the past. The 1957 Murray report in Australia, and the better-known 1963 Robbins report in Britain, established guidelines for university funding and access that gained wide political support for a generation. We can even suggest the level of funding that might be agreed now. In 2014 the average expenditure on higher education in OECD countries, from all sources, was 1.6 per cent of GDP. Poorer countries have less capacity, but that gives an order of magnitude that has some legitimacy.

We can do a lot with 1.6 per cent! But can the resources be got in a stable and equitable way? Private funding undermines organizational democracy, fair access, and research in the public interest; state funding risks policy reversals and centralization of power. We see all those effects today. I do not believe there is any economic formula that will *guarantee* stability and equity for ever; we have to rely on wider social changes too. Yet some funding mechanisms have better promise than others, and there are models available. The Chilean reform movement of 2011 is particularly interesting because privatization had gone so far in that country. The movement proposed to eradicate the profit motive from higher education and move funding to a needs basis. Concretely, it proposed that the state should pay for the education of the poorest 70 per cent of families, with guaranteed loans for the others. The system would be re-shaped by expanding and diversifying public universities, controlling increases in tuition, and enforcing the non-profit status of universities. In other countries too we can find useful mechanisms, such as public funding to universities through representative commissions rather than direct political control, and mixtures of central, regional and local government funding.[15]

Whatever the formula, only a university system with solid public respect is likely to gain a new compact. Public respect cannot be created by marketing. It will only be gained if universities respect each other, and if they offer real equity in access, creative teaching, consistent truthfulness, and tangible social engagement. The criteria for a good university and university system are not just blue-sky hopes, they are immediately relevant to the political process of change.

Most of the recent discussions of university reform have focussed on one country at a time, usually one in the global North. But all universities are embedded in a global economy of knowledge and are shaped by its inequalities. To end these inequalities is a vast, long-term project. We have made a start on the intellectual issues, through postcolonial critique, growing recognition of indigenous knowledge and Southern theory, and practical experience of South/South research links. We still have to tackle the issue of material redistribution, beyond the trickles of aid reaching universities in the global South.

At present we may even be going backwards, since the international market in fee-paying students sucks money out of developing countries to pay universities in richer ones. There may be a case for a Tobin tax on international fee payments (like the proposed tax on financial transactions) to return some funds to the countries of origin. But larger redistribution will be needed, which, again, depends on wider political and economic change.

Near the start of this book I quoted James Frazer's speculation in *The Golden Bough* that research-based science would some day be replaced by another, still unimagined, form of knowledge. I don't think we need to wait. In the multiple knowledge formations, practices and needs of the present, we already have the ingredients for a richer and stranger intellectual world.

Kartini Community University may not get funded; international agreement for a Childe Institute may never be reached; *university-b* may not come to pass. What will certainly continue, as long as human society does, is the need for organized knowledge and the capacity to make it grow. *University-a*, the university as we know it, has been the site of magnificent work in both teaching and research, which I have celebrated in this book. The same institution has been – and still is – the site of privilege, exclusion and exploitation on an appalling scale. That must be recognized too.

The workers and controllers of universities hold in trust a great collective resource. This is not really the bricks and mortar, nor the figures in university balance sheets. It is the vast intangible asset of organized knowledge: the archive, the investigations, the curricula, the teaching methods, the research know-how, and the situational knowledges and practical skills that bring the whole into existence. This is a powerful resource, immediately affecting hundreds of millions of people and through them the world. It is also vulnerable: it can be exploited, distorted or disrupted. It has to be made and re-made, daily and from generation to generation. Its future is not yet decided. I think it is possible to make that future creative, inclusive and democratic. It will require commitment and struggle. Good universities make the commitment and the struggle worthwhile.

Notes

Introduction

1 Readings 1996; Cooper, Hinkson & Sharp 2002; Ginsberg 2011.
2 Federal Reserve Bank of New York, *Quarterly Report on Household Debt and Credit*, February 2017, at www.newyorkfed.org/medialibrary/interactives/householdcredit/data/pdf/HHDC_2016Q4.pdf, accessed 10.10.2017.
3 United Nations, *Statistical Yearbook 2017*, at https://unstats.un.org/unsd/publications/statistical-yearbook/, accessed 27.02.2018; Marginson 2016.
4 Bok 2003, 2013, p. 408; Davis 2010, p. 123.
5 Sonnenberg 2017.
6 Sydney, Turney, Bygott & Chippendale 1991; Open University, Ferguson 1976; JNU, Batabyal 2014.
7 Sharma 2016.
8 Newman 1873 [1852].
9 Anderson 2004; on Berlin, Sweet 1980 vol. 2; on London, Davies & Bjarnason, 2013.
10 Bender 1993; Reuben 1996.
11 A wry survey of Australian university marketing slogans – not the worst examples I have ever seen – is in Kniest 2014.
12 For an admirable recent wish list see National Alliance for Public Universities 2014.

1 Making the knowledge: research

1 World Bank 2002; Mattelart 2003; Alvesson 2004.
2 Connell & Crawford 2007.
3 Mkandawire 2000, 2005.
4 For the emotional dimension of auditing, see Grant & Elizabeth 2015.
5 Harberd 2006, p. 238.

6 Darwin 1861 [1928], pp. 462–463. I have left out the middle of the paragraph, which is even more dramatic.
7 Connell 2006, p. 12.
8 Sharp & White 1968; Connell & Crawford 2007.
9 For the servants, Shapin 1994, ch. 8; for Bonnie, Connell & Wood 2002; for the autonomy scale, see Connell & Crawford 2007, pp. 198–200.
10 Pearson 1937, p. 21.
11 Popper 1959 [1934]; misleadingly titled in English *The Logic of Scientific Discovery*.
12 Feyerabend 1975, p. 10; Feynman 1992, p. 147.
13 Wootton 2016.
14 For an example of the idea that the humanities don't do research, see Collini 2012.
15 Pickering 1995.
16 Whittington 1975; for the significance of this study, see Gould 1991.
17 Einstein 1954, p. 126.
18 For the *DSM*, Zucker & Spitzer 2005; for Thucydides, Romilly 2012 [1956].
19 I cheerfully acknowledge my debt to Myles na Gopaleen's critique of Einstein: O'Nolan 2007 pp. 96–99.
20 For a clear and extended example of such work, see the survey of research on sub-Antarctic freshwater invertebrates by Dartnall 2017.
21 On the printing press, Wootton 2016, pp. 301ff.; Linear B, Robinson 2002, pp. 102ff.; the Platonic dialogue, Kagamé 1956. Ware & Mabe 2015, in an industry report on academic journals, credibly give 28 100 'active scholarly peer-reviewed English-language journals', and 6450 non-English-language journals, in 2014.
22 Comte 1830–1842.
23 Frazer 1922 edition, p. 712.
24 An excellent account is given by Holloway 1996.
25 Text and translation of Nobel's will: www.nobelprize.org/alfred_nobel/will/will-full.html, accessed 25.06.2017.
26 Connell & Crawford 2007, pp. 192–193; Kuhn 1970 [first edn 1962], ch. 3.
27 I take this idea from the discussion of ontoformativity in Karel Kosík's forgotten masterpiece *Dialectics of the Concrete* (1976).
28 Connell & Wood 2002, p. 177.
29 Hutchins 1936, passim.
30 *Mathematical Review* and *Zentralblatt für Mathematik*, *MSC2010*, at www.ams.org/mathscinet/msc/pdfs/classifications2010.pdf, accessed 15.03.2017.

31 For motor cars, Wace 1977.
32 Daston and Galison 2007; for problems in defining truth, Rorty & Engel 2007, Tarski 1956 [1931]; on truth and human rights, UN General Assembly 68/165 of 18 December 2013.
33 Shapin 1994; Hudson 1972.
34 See the useful discussion of the knowledge commons in Münch 2014.
35 Pashler & Wagenmakers 2012.
36 Lamont 2009.
37 On Stapel, see the careful account by Stroebe, Postmes & Spears 2012; on Burt, see Kamin 1974, and many others.
38 On drug research, Lundh et al. 2012; on Irving's distortions of history, Evans 2002; on gay parenting, Stacey 2011, p. 195; on the attacks against evolutionary biology, Selkirk & Burrows 1987.
39 Evans 2002, pp. 252–72. See also his book *In Defence of History* (1997). I find Evans' realism more convincing than the curious defence by Latour 2004, which seems to allow realism to physical science but not social science.
40 Lukács 1971; Harding 2008.

2 Learning and teaching

1 University of Córdoba Students Federation 1918.
2 Little 1970.
3 Srigley 2015; Hil 2015, p. 89.
4 Collini 2017, p. 107.
5 On solitude in writing, Gordimer 1975, pp. 11–12.
6 Pioneering studies are Ehrenreich & English 1973, Goodson 1988.
7 Holland & Eisenhart 1990.
8 For this process at the Open University, Ferguson 1976.
9 Giraud 2014, p. 135.
10 SAT was formerly the Scholastic Aptitude Test, ACT American College Testing, GRE Graduate Record Examination; the TOEFL is for English language skills. For the ongoing US controversy about bias in these tests see Santelices & Wilson 2010.
11 Power 1999.
12 Student critique, Johnson 1969; feminism, Crowley & Himmelweit 1992; White curriculum, Peters 2015; South Africa, Shay & Peseta 2016; indigenous knowledge, Aikman & King 2012; Kaupapa Māori, Walker, Eketone & Gibbs 2006.
13 For a useful survey of this rather confused research, see the papers in Barnett 2005.

14 Freire 1996, p. 53.
15 For enrolment numbers, see ICEF Monitor 2016.
16 Harvard Business School 2018.
17 Van der Veer & Valsiner 1991, pp. 336–348; for application in a university zoology course, Harland 2003.
18 Connell & Manathunga 2012.
19 Bagelman & Bagelman 2016.

3 The collective intellectual: university workers

1 Connell 2011, ch. 6.
2 For the broad historical and global story, see Pietsch 2013, Welch 2005.
3 Szekeres 2011; Sebalt, Holbrook & Bourke 2012; Whitchurch 2008.
4 Ferguson 1976.
5 Graham 2012, among the very few close-focus studies of this linking, shows how new 'learning spaces' such as Facebook pages become effective through the work of operations staff, who have to teach the students how to use university systems.
6 Graham 2012, p. 448.
7 Crothers 1991, p. 335.
8 Statistics from: Larkins 2012; Universities Australia 2015; Sebalt, Holbrook & Bourke 2012. For recently released gender data from the National Autonomous University of Mexico see Secretaría de Igualdad 2018.
9 Krücken, Blümel & Kloke 2013; Larkins 2012; Szekeres 2011.
10 University of Cape Town 2015.
11 Peetz, Strachan & Troup 2014, Winchester & Browning 2015; for 'good men', Ross 1966, p. 78.
12 Becher 1989. The second edition, Becher & Trowler 2001, has a new section on 'Women's academic careers'; it has no section on 'Men's academic careers', which are still taken for granted as the norm.
13 Tancred-Sheriff 1985.
14 On 'gender theory', Garbagnoli & Prearo 2017. On the fascinating Novikoff story, Holmes 1989. It's currently impossible to get the precise number of academics targeted by the Erdoğan government.
15 Alvesson 2004; for a remarkable early analysis of this issue, see Sharp & White 1968.
16 Schwartz 2014, p. 512; May, Peetz & Strahan 2013; Andrews et al. 2016. For a careful integration of different sources, and analysis of the official concealment, see Dados, Goodman & Yasukawa 2018, and data presented by these authors at www.scholarlyteaching.net.

17 Andrews et al. 2016, pp. 10–11.
18 For the teaching focus of for-profit private universities in the United States, Tierney & Hentschke 2007; in Chile, Bellei, Cabalin & Orellana 2014; in India, Gupta 2016.
19 *Wealth of Nations*, Book I Chapter viii.
20 Williams 1965. The story is set in a second-tier college in the American midwest.
21 Acker & Feuerverger 1996.
22 Rothengatter & Hil 2013; Andrews et al. 2016; on *Profesores TAXI*, Santos 2006; Kimber & Ehrich 2015.
23 Morgan & Wood 2017; cf. Brown, Goodman & Yasukawa 2010.
24 Pick, Teo & Yeung 2012; Tytherleigh et al. 2005, p. 54.
25 Altbach 1997.
26 For a grim picture of teaching in provincial India, Jayaram 2011.
27 Gupta 2016; Jansen 2017.

4 The global economy of knowledge

1 Arabic numerals in turn derived from India and the notation for zero possibly comes from South-east Asia: Nanda 2016, ch. 2.
2 Hountondji 1997.
3 Darwin 1845: I give the title of the second edition. For background, McCalman 2009.
4 Branagan & Vallance 1981.
5 Usher 2017 is an excellent short history of global ranking systems.
6 Connell et al. 2017.
7 Tierney & Kan 2016, p. 1781.
8 For a useful short history, Agarwal 2007.
9 Pietsch 2013.
10 Hanafi 2011; Odora Hoppers 2002.
11 Ishikawa 2012; Choi 2010.
12 Indian figures, Gaikwad & Solunke 2013; for JNU, Batabyal 2014; for a state-level university, Dongerkery 1966; for Australia, Forsyth 2014.
13 Hountondji 1973; Mazrui 1975; wa Thiong'o 1986, 1993.
14 US foundations, Berman 1983; Nigeria, Johnson 1966; for such a trajectory, Hountondji 2002.
15 Caribbean medical schools, Harris 2013; student numbers, Center for Academic Mobility Research 2014.
16 On NYU's overseas expansion, Ross 2009.
17 For the dodgy methodology, read the ranking agencies' own explanations, e.g. The Times Higher 2005; for the underlying logic,

Shahjahan & Morgan 2016; for the history and the dirty politics, Usher 2017.

18 On China, Rhoads et al. 2014, esp. p. 153; on Singapore, Qi 2015, p. 340.

19 Goodson & Ball 1984.

20 Connell 2007; Steinmetz 2013, part I.

21 Connell & Wood 2002.

22 Hernándes Bringas et al. 2015.

23 Schiebinger & Swan 2005; Axelby 2008.

24 For the *Australopithecus* story, Dart 1959.

25 Jian Liu 2012; Mkandawire 2000, 2005; Bennett 2008, p. 7.

26 Vessuri 2003, p. 271.

27 For survey data on such links see Welch 2005; Connell, Wood & Crawford 2005.

28 Connell et al. 2017.

29 Lillis & Curry 2010, p. 135.

30 Somerville & Perkins 2010; see also Odora Hoppers 2002 and many other accounts.

31 Lal 2002; for alternatives in the Arabic world, South and South-east Asia, see Alatas 2006.

32 wa Thiong'o 1986, pp. 94–101; Santos 2014; Luckett 2016; Bakare-Yusuf 2003; wa Thiong'o 1993, p. 29.

33 Bulbeck 1998; Lugones 2010; Roberts & Connell 2016.

34 Adriansen, Madsen & Jensen 2016, ch. 7. The classic statement is Smith 1999.

35 For background, Alperin, Fischman & Willinsky 2011.

5 Privilege machines

1 Raffe 1977; Higher Education Council, Australia 1996, p. 45; Council on Higher Education, South Africa 2016; Buckner 2014; Kwiek 2014. For a useful global summary of statistics of unequal access, see UNESCO 2017.

2 Chankseliani 2014; compare the English case in Whitty, Hayton & Tang 2015.

3 Marginson 2016, p. 422; Breier 2010.

4 Bernstein 1971; Bourdieu 1966.

5 Parkin 1979; for this approach to US universities, Subramaniam, Perrucci & Whitlock 2012. On massification, Altbach, Reisberg & Rumbley 2009.

6 Slaughter & Leslie 1997; Münch 2014.

7 Anderson 2004, p. 250.
8 Australia, Macintyre, Brett & Croucher 2017; China, Rhoads et al. 2014, p. 121.
9 For schools, Connell et al. 1982, Kenway et al. 2017; for universities, Xiang 2009.
10 On credentials, Collins 1979, whose treatment is effectively a theory of social closure.
11 On schools, Connell et al. 1982, Madrid 2016. On European universities, Anderson 2004.
12 See for instance the syllabus of the MBA at the University of Ruhuna in Sri Lanka, at: www.mgt.ruh.ac.lk/mba/files/MBA_HAND_BOOK.pdf, accessed 18.04.2018.
13 China, Rhoads et al. 2014; Bulgaria, Boyadjieva 2014; Poland, Kwiek 2014; Konrád & Szelényi 1979.
14 For a sharp analysis of Harvard's strategies, see Trumpbour 1989.
15 For the 'world class' rhetoric, David 2016; for the irrationality of the 'excellence initiative', Münch 2014.
16 Higher Education Council, Australia 1996; Wankhede 2016.
17 Rosenberg 1982.
18 Anderson 2004, pp. 256–273.
19 For the spectrum of women's studies in the metropole, Crowley & Himmelweit 1992.
20 Probert 2005, and for an update with more stress on insecure employment, Peetz, Strachan & Troup 2014; for students, Australian Human Rights Commission 2017; for the survey of Africa, Mama & Barnes 2007.
21 Muhr 2016 compares the Venezuelan and Brazilian approaches; Robinson & Meerkotter 2003 document one of the anti-apartheid struggles.
22 Rama 2012; for the policy environment in India, Gupta 2016.
23 Tharu 2016.
24 Raju, Shastri & Banyal 2017.
25 Matthew 25, verse 29. This is actually a religious metaphor, not an endorsement of wealth!
26 For humanism among operations staff specifically, see Lawless 2017.

6 The university business

1 For universities under an earlier generation of business men, see the brilliant polemic by Veblen 1918.
2 For neoliberalism and its geopolitics, Dados & Connell 2018.

3 Ernst & Young Australia, 2012, p. 27, a fine example of banal corporate thought about universities.

4 Hanover Research website www.hanoverresearch.com, accessed 13.02.2018.

5 For the corporations involved, Rama 2012, Robertson & Olds 2017.

6 For the presidential view, Bok 2003, Davis 2017, Jansen 2017; for one example of World Bank influence, Mamdani 2009; Mönckeberg 2013; for the continent-wide impact on Latin American universities, see Brunner 2007.

7 Kumar 2013; for Chhattisgarh, Gupta 2016.

8 McPhee 2014.

9 Matasar's article now at http://heinonline.org/HOL/LandingPage?handle=hein.journals/uflr48&div=44&id=&page=, quoted in Ward 2012, p. 105. On the human capital assumption, see McGettigan 2015. On Finland, see Välimaa 2012.

10 Broad surveys include Parker 2011, Ward 2012; for country studies, see Santos 2006 (Chile), Thornton 2015 (Australia), Radice 2013 (Britain), Gupta 2016 (India); for ethnographies see Tuchman 2009, Thornton 2012, Mamdani 2009.

11 Charles Sturt University 2015. Amounts of money are in AUD. The figure for staff is 'Full-time Equivalent', so the actual number of people will be larger.

12 For the complaint by Huiqing Jin, president of one of the private universities, http://science.sciencemag.org/content/346/6208/401.full, accessed 18.04.2018.

13 Tierney & Hentschke 2007; for India, Gupta 2016.

14 Anderson 2004, Xiang 2009. The process in elite private schools is not identical: see Madrid 2016, Kenway et al. 2017.

15 That is how the statement read in early 2017. It was evidently too blunt. The mission statement has since been re-written to emphasize that commodification is really about benefit to society! See www.enterprise.cam.ac.uk/who-we-are/our-mission/, accessed 24.09.2017.

16 Powell & Owen-Smith 2002.

17 Slaughter & Leslie 1997.

18 Larivière, Haustein & Mongeon 2015.

19 Szekeres 2011, Parker 2011, Lorenz 2012, are among those who note the change of language.

20 Davis 2010, p. 97.

21 Parker 2014.

22 Krücken, Blümel & Kloke 2013.

23 EAB website at www.eab.com/, accessed 13.02.2018; World Academic Summit website at www.theworldsummitseries.com, accessed 13.02.2018.
24 Blackmore & Sawers 2015; Wajcman 1998.
25 Schwartz 2014, p. 515; Jansen 2017. The expansion of management numbers is noted by Ginsberg 2011, Warner 2015.
26 Power 1999; in universities, Parker 2011, Grant & Elizabeth 2015, Welch 2016. The estimate for British quality assurance is in Holmwood et al. 2016, p. 28.
27 Williamson 2018.
28 Symes 1996; and almost any current university website.
29 Santos 2006, pp. 6–7; for Rahman on Western Sydney University, visit www.youtube.com/watch?v=5Bg90nkRL3c.
30 For fake accountability and gaming, Radice 2013, Lynch 2015, and many others.
31 There is, naturally, little documentation of this, but see Anderson 2008.
32 Warner 2015, p. 3.
33 Ginsberg 2011; Pulido 2014.
34 The Lord Chancellor was Edward Thurlow. I quote the pungent popular version of his remark; the written report was tamer.
35 Cain and Hewitt 2004; Gupta 2016.
36 Radice 2013, p. 415; see also Slaughter & Leslie 1997, Parker 2011, Lynch 2015.
37 Sturm & Turner 2011; Naidoo 2016.
38 Mamdani 2009; Welch 2017; Jian Liu 2012.
39 For an illuminating account of this process in India, Krishna & Patra 2016.
40 Gill 2010.
41 Anderson 2008; Warner 2015; Sánchez Lopera & Rueda Ortiz 2014.
42 For Chile, Bellei, Cabalin and Orellana 2014; for Newcastle, Morrish & Analogue University Writing Collective 2017; for detail on the 2018 strike, 'The 2018 USS strike: UCU and UUK', at www.libguides.ioe.ac.uk/ussstrike2018/ucuanduuk, accessed 15.04.2018.
43 Schwartz 2014; Marginson 2006; Ward 2012; Radice 2013; Jansen 2017; Lorenz 2012; Smith 2012; Thornton 2015; Hil 2015; Tuchman 2009; Collini 2012, 2017; NTEU Sydney University Branch 2015; Watts 2017. For management responses, Bok 2003, ch. 2; Thrift 2016.

7 Universities of hope

1 For this perspective on global links, Hobson 2004.

2 For Chinese science, Needham 1954, though note the Eurocentric problematic. For knowledge in a contemporary Aboriginal community, Somerville & Perkins 2010.

3 Dutta & Robinson 1996; Jha 1994; Das Gupta 2004. Website www.visvabharati.ac.in/, accessed 29.09.2017.

4 Shariati 1986.

5 Pszenicki 1979; Genell & Kostera 1996.

6 Ross 1966 is an amazing collection of vice-chancellors' accounts; for the Open University, Ferguson 1976. For retrospects see Pellew 2014 (Britain), Batabyal 2014 (JNU), Connell & Manathunga 2012 (Macquarie). Robinson & Meerkotter 2003 describe a similar approach at the University of the Western Cape.

7 Lichtman 1973; Wolpman 2017 (Midpeninsula); Johnson 1969 (Sydney).

8 Reed 2013; for the current programme, www.ccny.cuny.edu/seek.

9 Ivancheva 2013; Muhr 2010; McCowan 2016.

10 RUIICAY 2012.

11 Hau'ofa 2008; Smith 1997, 1999; Lopes Cardozo 2012.

12 Hountondji 1997; Melgarejo 2015; on the relation with law, Younging 2015.

13 Al-Afghani 1968; on Islamic science, Ghamari-Tabrizi 1996; Hanafi 2011.

14 Zeghal 2007, p. 119; Brown 2011; statistics in Buckner 2014; for broad background, Hourani 1991; for current problems of authority and curriculum, Bano 2017.

15 See www.global-labour-university.org/341.html.

16 For *Arena*, Hinkson et al. 2016; website at http://arena.org.au/. For a beautiful description of *Manushi*'s founding, Kishwar & Vanita 1984.

17 Free University of New York City 2013; for Brisbane, https://brisbanefreeuniversity.org/.

18 See www.danishfolkhighschools.com/; www.folkuniversitetet.se.

19 Lindqvist 1978.

20 Richards 2016; Kippax et al. 1993.

21 For the BAA Observing Community https://britastro.org/community. For a short introduction to citizen science, https://theconversation.com/explainer-what-is-citizen-science-16487; for an exoplanet, Norris 2017.

22 Precarias a la deriva 2018; Wadsworth 1984.

23 Berg & Seeber 2016; another nice argument for 'slow scholarship' is Mountz et al. 2015.
24 For a helpful introduction to the movement, Morrison 2015; for Latin America, Alperin, Fischman & Willinsky 2011.
25 For Sci-Hub go to http://sci-hub.io/.
26 www.edx.org, accessed 15.03.2018.
27 www.freedomuniversitygeorgia.com, accessed 13.02.2018.
28 Fanon 1968; Shariati 1981; Harding 2008.
29 Oldfield 2015; compare Cresswell & Spandler 2013, on activism and psychiatry.
30 Ferguson 1976, chs 3 and 5.

8 The good university

1 E.g. Ernst & Young 2012.
2 Kenway & Fahey 2009.
3 Budgets in dollar terms, for universities of about the same size. For research funding, Adriansen, Madsen & Jensen 2016.
4 Treanor 2006.
5 Kenway, Boden & Fahey 2015; there is more in this collection, Thornton 2015.
6 Mbembe 2016.
7 Halffman & Radder 2015.
8 Lem 1970 [1961]; Le Guin 1974.
9 Kartini is a national heroine in Indonesia. For her writings in English translation, Kartini 2014. There is a real Universitas Kartini in Surabaya, a small private college set up during General Suharto's New Order regime. No reference to this college is intended.
10 Mistral 2010, p. 447. Clunky translation by Raewyn Connell, with some assistance from Ursula Le Guin's translation.
11 For the importance of new groups entering universities, Clegg 2016.
12 On the right to higher education, McCowan 2012.
13 For this tension in authoritarian China, Xiang Biao 2009.
14 See the discussion of a 'knowledge satyagraha' in Vidya Ashram 2009.
15 For the Chilean movement's proposals, Bellei, Cabalin & Orellana 2014.

References

Acker, Sandra and Grace Feuerverger. 1996. Doing good and feeling bad: The work of women university teachers. *Cambridge Journal of Education*, vol. 26 no. 3, pp. 401–422.

Adriansen, Hanne Kirstine, Lene Møller Madsen and Stig Jensen (eds). 2016. *Higher Education and Capacity Building in Africa: The Geography and Power of Knowledge under Changing Conditions.* London: Routledge.

Agarwal, Pawan. 2007. Higher education in India: Growth, concerns, and change agenda. *Higher Education Quarterly*, vol. 61 no. 2, pp. 197–207.

Aikman, Sheila and Linda King. 2012. Indigenous knowledge and education. *Compare: A Journal of Comparative and International Education*, vol. 42 no. 5, pp. 673–681.

Al-Afghani, Sayyid Jamal ad-Din. 1968 [1881]. Refutation of the Materialists, pp. 130–174 in *An Islamic Response to Imperialism: Political and Religious Writings of Sayyid Jamal ad-Din 'al-Afghani'.* Trans. Nikki R. Keddie and Hamid Algar. Berkeley, CA: University of California Press.

Alatas, Syed Farid. 2006. *Alternative Discourses in Asian Social Science: Responses to Eurocentrism.* New Delhi: Sage.

Alperin, Juan Pablo, Gustavo E. Fischman and John Willinsky. 2011. Scholarly communication strategies in Latin America's Research-intensive Universities. *Revista educación superior y sociedad*, vol. 16 no. 2. Online at ess.iesalc.unesco.org.ve/index.php/article/view/409/347.

Altbach, Philip G. 1997. An international academic crisis? The American professoriate in comparative perspective. *Daedalus*, Fall, vol. 126 no. 4, pp. 315–338.

Altbach, Philip G., Liz Reisberg and Laura E. Rumbley. 2009. *Trends in Global Higher Education: Tracking an Academic Revolution.* A report prepared for the UNESCO World Conference on Higher Education. Paris: UNESCO.

Alvesson, Mats. 2004. *Knowledge Work and Knowledge-intensive Firms.* Oxford: Oxford University Press.

Anderson, Gina. 2008. Mapping academic resistance in the managerial university. *Organization*, vol. 15 no. 2, pp. 251–270.

Anderson, R. D. 2004. *European Universities from the Enlightenment to 1914*. Oxford: Oxford University Press.

Andrews, Stuart, Liz Bare, Peter Bentley, Leo Goedegebuure, Catherine Pugsley and Bianca Rice. 2016. *Contingent Academic Employment in Australian Universities*. Discussion paper. Melbourne: L. H. Martin Institute.

Australian Human Rights Commission. 2017. *Change the Course: National Report on Sexual Assault and Sexual Harassment at Australian Universities, August 2017*. Sydney: Australian Human Rights Commission.

Axelby, Richard. 2008. Calcutta Botanic Garden and the colonial re-ordering of the Indian environment. *Archives of Natural History*, vol. 35 no. 1, pp. 150–163.

Bagelman, Jen and Carly Bagelman. 2016. Zines: Crafting change and repurposing the neoliberal university. *ACME: An International Journal for Critical Geographies*, vol. 15 no. 2, pp. 365–392.

Bakare-Yusuf, Bibi. 2003. 'Yorubas don't do gender': A critical review of Oyeronke Oyewumi's *The Invention of Women: Making an African Sense of Western Gender Discourses. African Identities*, no. 1, pp. 121–143.

Bano, Masooda. 2017. At the tipping point? Al-Azhar's growing crisis of moral authority. *International Journal of Middle East Studies*, in press.

Barnett, Ronald (ed.). 2005. *Reshaping the University: New Relationships between Research, Scholarship and Teaching*. Maidenhead: Open University Press.

Batabyal, Rakesh. 2014. *JNU: The Making of a University*. Noida, UP: HarperCollins.

Becher, Tony. 1989. *Academic Tribes and Territories: Intellectual Enquiry and the Culture of Disciplines*. Buckingham: Society for Research into Higher Education and Open University Press. 2nd edition, Tony Becher and Paul. R. Trowler, 2001.

Bellei, Cristián, Cristian Cabalin and Victor Orellana. 2014. The university student movement against neoliberal educational policies: The 2011 Chilean student mobilisations. *Studies in Higher Education*, vol. 39 no. 3, pp. 426–440.

Benda, Julien. 1928. *The Great Betrayal (La Trahison des Clercs)*. Trans. Richard Aldington. London: Routledge.

Bender, Thomas. 1993. *Intellect and Public Life: Essays on the Social History of Academic Intellectuals in the United States*. Baltimore, MD: Johns Hopkins University Press.

Bennett, Jane. 2008. Editorial. Researching for life: Paradigms and power. *Feminist Africa*, no. 11, pp. 1–12.

Berg, Maggie and Barbara K. Seeber. 2016. *The Slow Professor: Challenging the Culture of Speed in the Academy*. Toronto: University of Toronto Press.

Berman, Edward H. 1983. *The Influence of the Carnegie, Ford and Rockefeller Foundations on American Foreign Policy*. Albany, NY: State University of New York Press.

Bernstein, Basil. 1971. *Class, Codes and Control*. London: Routledge & Kegan Paul.

Blackmore, Jill and Naarah Sawers. 2015. Executive power and scaled-up gender subtexts in Australian entrepreneurial universities. *Gender and Education*, vol. 27 no. 3, pp. 320–337.

Bok, Derek. 2003. *Universities in the Marketplace: The Commercialization of Higher Education*. Princeton, NJ: Princeton University Press.

Bok, Derek. 2013. *Higher Education in America*. Princeton, NJ: Princeton University Press.

Bourdieu, Pierre. 1966. L'école conservatrice. *Revue française de sociologie*, vol. 7, pp. 325–347.

Boyadjieva, Pepka Alexandrova. 2014. Admissions policies as a mechanism for social engineering: The case of the Bulgarian communist regime, pp. 143–166 in Anna Mountford-Zimdars, Daniel Sabbagh and David Post (eds), *Fair Access to Higher Education: Global Perspectives*. Chicago, IL: University of Chicago Press.

Branagan, D. F. and T. G. Vallance. 1981. David, Sir Tannatt William Edgeworth (1858–1934). *Australian Dictionary of Biography*, vol. 8. Online at http://adb.anu.edu.au/biography/david-sir-tannatt-william-edgeworth-5894/text10033, accessed 5 August 2018.

Breier, Mignonne. 2010. From 'financial considerations' to 'poverty': Towards a reconceptualization of the role of finances in higher education student drop out. *Higher Education*, vol. 60, pp. 657–670.

Brown, Nathan J. 2011. Post-revolutionary Al-Azhar. 'The Carnegie Papers' series. Washington DC: Carnegie Endowment for International Peace.

Brown, Tony, James Goodman and Keiko Yasukawa. 2010. Academic casualization in Australia: Class divisions in the university. *Journal of Industrial Relations*, vol. 52 no. 2, pp. 169–182.

Brunner, José Joaquín. 2007. *Universidad y sociedad en América Latina*. 2nd edition. Xalapa, Veracruz: Universidad Veracruzana.

Buckner, Elizabeth. 2014. Access to higher education in Egypt: Examining trends by university sector, pp. 167–192 in Anna Mountford-Zimdars, Daniel Sabbagh and David Post (eds),

Fair Access to Higher Education: Global Perspectives. Chicago, IL: University of Chicago Press.

Bulbeck, Chilla. 1998. *Re-Orienting Western Feminisms: Women's Diversity in a Postcolonial World*. Cambridge: Cambridge University Press.

Cain, John and John Hewitt. 2004. *Off Course: From Public Place to Marketplace at Melbourne University*. Melbourne: Scribe Publications.

Center for Academic Mobility Research, Institute of International Education. 2014. *Project Atlas: Trends and Global Data 2014*. n.p.

Chankseliani, Maia. 2014. Rural disadvantage in Georgian higher education admissions: A mixed-methods study, pp. 66–97 in Anna Mountford-Zimdars, Daniel Sabbagh and David Post (eds), *Fair Access to Higher Education*. Chicago, IL: University of Chicago Press.

Charles Sturt University. 2015. *Annual Report 2014*. Bathurst: Charles Sturt University. Online at www.csu.edu.au/about/publications.

Choi, Po King. 2010. 'Weep for Chinese university': A case study of English hegemony and academic capitalism in higher education in Hong Kong. *Journal of Education Policy*, vol. 25 no. 2, pp. 233–252.

Clegg, Sue. 2016. The necessity and possibility of powerful 'regional' knowledge: Curriculum change and renewal. *Teaching in Higher Education*, vol. 21 no. 4, pp. 457–470.

Collini, Stefan. 2012. *What Are Universities For?* London: Penguin.

Collini, Stefan. 2017. *Speaking of Universities*. London: Verso.

Collins, Randall. 1979. *The Credential Society: A Historical Sociology of Education and Stratification*. New York: Academic Press.

Comte, Auguste. 1975 [1830–42]. *Cours de philosophie positive*. Extracts translated in Gertrud Lenzer (ed.), *Auguste Comte and Positivism: The Essential Writings*. New York: Harper Torchbooks, pp. 71–306.

Connell, Raewyn. 2006. Core activity: Reflexive intellectual workers and cultural crisis. *Journal of Sociology*, vol. 42 no. 1, pp. 5–23.

Connell, Raewyn. 2007. *Southern Theory: The Global Dynamics of Knowledge in Social Science*. Sydney: Allen & Unwin Australia.

Connell, Raewyn. 2011. *Confronting Equality: Gender, Knowledge and Global Change*. Cambridge: Polity.

Connell, Raewyn and June Crawford. 2007. Mapping the intellectual labour process. *Journal of Sociology*, vol. 43 no. 2, pp. 187–205.

Connell, Raewyn and Catherine Manathunga. 2012. On doctoral education: How to supervise a PhD, 1985–2011. *Australian Universities Review*, vol. 54 no. 1, pp. 5–9.

Connell, Raewyn and Julian Wood. 2002. Globalization and scientific labour: Patterns in a life-history study of intellectual workers in the periphery. *Journal of Sociology*, vol. 38 no. 2, pp. 167–190.

Connell, Raewyn, Julian Wood and June Crawford. 2005. The global connections of intellectual workers: An Australian study. *International Sociology*, vol. 20 no. 1, pp. 5–26.

Connell, Raewyn, Dean Ashenden, Sandra Kessler and Gary Dowsett. 1982. *Making the Difference: Schools, Families and Social Division.* Sydney: Allen & Unwin Australia.

Connell, Raewyn, Rebecca Pearse, Fran Collyer, João Maia and Robert Morrell. 2017. Re-making the global economy of knowledge: Do new fields of research change the structure of North–South relations? *British Journal of Sociology*, published online August 2017, DOI: 10.1111/1468-4446.12294.

Cooper, Simon, John Hinkson and Geoff Sharp (eds). 2002. *Scholars and Entrepreneurs: The Universities in Crisis.* Melbourne: Arena.

Council on Higher Education, South Africa. 2016. *South African Higher Education Reviewed: Two Decades of Democracy.* Pretoria: CHE.

Cresswell, Mark and Helen Spandler. 2013. The engaged academic: Academic intellectuals and the psychiatric survivor movement. *Social Movement Studies*, vol. 12 no. 2, pp. 138–154.

Crothers, Charles. 1991. The internal structure of sociology departments: The role of graduate students and other groups. *Teaching Sociology*, vol. 19, pp. 333–343.

Crowley, Helen and Susan Himmelweit. 1992. *Knowing Women: Feminism and Knowledge.* Cambridge: Polity.

Dados, Nour and Raewyn Connell. 2018. Neoliberalism in world perspective: Southern origins and Southern dynamics, pp. 28–39 in Damien Cahill, Melinda Cooper, Martijn Konings and David Primrose (eds), *The Sage Handbook of Neoliberalism.* London: Sage.

Dados, Nour, James Goodman and Keiko Yasukawa. 2018. Counting the uncounted. Unpublished draft.

Dart, Raymond A. 1959. *Adventures with the Missing Link.* New York: Harper.

Dartnall, Herbert J. G. 2017. The freshwater fauna of the south polar region: A 140-year review. *Papers and Proceedings of the Royal Society of Tasmania*, vol. 151, pp. 19–57.

Darwin, Charles. n.d. [1845]. *Journal of Researches into the Natural History and Geology of the Countries Visited during the Voyage of H.M.S. 'Beagle' Round the World.* 2nd edition. London: Ward, Lock & Co.

Darwin, Charles. 1861 [1928]. *On the Origin of Species by Means of Natural Selection, or the Preservation of Favoured Races in the Struggle for Life.* New edition. New York: D. Appleton and Company.

Das Gupta, Uma. 2004. *Rabindranath Tagore: A Biography.* New Delhi: Oxford University Press.

Daston, Lorraine and Peter Galison. 2007. *Objectivity*. New York: Zone Books.

David, Matthew. 2016. Fabricated world class: Global university league tables, status differentiation and myths of global competition. *British Journal of Sociology of Education*, vol. 37 no. 1, pp. 169–189.

Davies, Graeme and Svava Bjarnason. 2013. After empire: The 'London model' transformed since the Second World War, pp. 27–40 in Deryck M. Schreuder (ed.), *Universities for a New World*. New Delhi: Sage and Association of Commonwealth Universities.

Davis, Glyn. 2010. *The Republic of Learning: Higher Education Transforms Australia. Boyer Lecture Series 2010*. Sydney: HarperCollins.

Davis, Glyn. 2017. *The Australian Idea of a University*. Melbourne: Melbourne University Press.

Dongerkery, S. R. 1966. Marathwada University, pp. 105–120 in Murray G. Ross (ed.), *New Universities in the Modern World*. London: Macmillan.

Dutta, Krishna and Andrew Robinson. 1996. *Rabindranath Tagore: The Myriad-Minded Man*. New York: St Martin's Press.

Ehrenreich, Barbara and Deidre English. 1973. *Witches, Midwives, and Nurses: A History of Women Healers*. 2nd edition. Old Westbury, NY: The Feminist Press.

Einstein, Albert. 1954 [1916]. *Relativity: The Special and the General Theory*. Trans. Robert W. Lawson. 15th edition. Abingdon: Routledge.

Ernst & Young. 2012. *University of the Future: A Thousand Year Old Industry on the Cusp of Profound Change*. Ernst and Young, Australia.

Evans, Richard J. 1997. *In Defence of History*. London: Granta.

Evans, Richard J. 2002. *Telling Lies about Hitler: The Holocaust, History and the David Irving Trial*. London: Verso.

Fanon, Frantz. 1968. *The Wretched of the Earth*. New York: Grove Press.

Federal Reserve Bank of New York. 2017. *Quarterly Report on Household Debt and Credit*, February. Online at www.newyorkfed.org/medialibrary/interactives/householdcredit/data/pdf/HHDC_2016Q4.pdf, accessed 13 October 2017.

Ferguson, John. 1976. *The Open University from Within*. New York: New York University Press.

Feyerabend, Paul. 1975. *Against Method: Outline of an Anarchistic Theory of Knowledge*. London: New Left Books.

Feynman, Richard P. 1992 [1965]. *The Character of Physical Law*. London: Penguin.

Forsyth, Hannah. 2014. *A History of the Modern Australian University*. Sydney: New South Books.

Frazer, James. 1993 [1922]. *The Golden Bough: A Study in Magic and Religion.* Abridged edition. Ware: Wordsworth.

Free University of New York City. 2013. *How to Free U.* Online at www.freeuniversitynyc.org/files/2013/How-To-Free-U-email-format-edited-1.pdf.

Freire, Paulo. 1996. *Pedagogy of the Oppressed.* London: Penguin.

Gaikwad, B. R. and R. S. Solunke. 2013. Growth of higher education in India. *International Research Journal of Social Sciences,* vol. 2 no. 8, pp. 58–60.

Garbagnoli, Sara and Massimo Prearo. 2017. *La croisade 'anti-genre': Du Vatican aux manifs pour tous.* Paris: Textuel.

Genell, Kristina and Monika Kostera. 1996. The Flying University: Institutional transformation in Poland, pp. 226–246 in M. M. Lee, Hugo Letiche, Robert Crawshaw and Michael Thomas (eds), *Management Education in the New Europe: Boundaries and Complexity.* London: International Thompson.

Ghamari-Tabrizi, Behrooz. 1996. Is Islamic science possible? *Social Epistemology,* vol. 10 no. 3–4, pp. 317–330.

Gill, Rosalind. 2010. Breaking the silence: The hidden injuries of neo-liberal academia, pp. 228–244 in Róisín Flood and Rosalind Gill (eds), *Secrecy and Silence in the Research Process: Feminist Reflections.* London: Routledge.

Ginsberg, Benjamin. 2011. *The Fall of the Faculty: The Rise of the All-Administrative University and Why It Matters.* New York: Oxford University Press.

Giraud, Yann. 2014. Negotiating the 'middle-of-the-road' position: Paul Samuelson, MIT, and the politics of textbook writing, 1945–55. *History of Political Economy,* vol. 46, annual supplement, pp. 134–152.

Goodson, Ivor F. 1988. *The Making of Curriculum: Collected Essays.* London: Falmer Press.

Goodson, Ivor and Stephen J. Ball. 1984. *Defining the Curriculum: Histories and Ethnographies.* London: Falmer Press.

Gordimer, Nadine. 1975. *Selected Stories.* London: Jonathan Cape.

Gould, Stephen Jay. 1991. *Wonderful Life: The Burgess Shale and the Nature of History.* London: Penguin.

Graham, Carroll. 2012. Transforming spaces and identities: The contributions of professional staff to learning spaces in higher education. *Journal of Higher Education Policy and Management,* vol. 34 no. 4, pp. 437–452.

Grant, Barbara M. and Vivienne Elizabeth. 2015. Unpredictable feelings: Academic women under research audit. *British Educational Research Journal,* vol. 41 no. 2, pp. 287–302.

Gupta, Asha. 2016. Emerging trends in private higher education in India, pp. 355–374 in N. V. Varghese and Malik Garima (eds), *India Higher Education Report 2015*. London: Routledge.

Halffman, Willem and Hans Radder. 2015. The academic manifesto: From an occupied to a public university. *Minerva*, vol. 53, pp. 165–187.

Hanafi, Sari. 2011. University systems in the Arab East: Publish globally and perish locally vs publish locally and perish globally. *Current Sociology*, vol. 59 no. 3, pp. 291–309.

Hanover Research. 2018. Website www.hanoverresearch.com, accessed 13 February 2018.

Harberd, Nicholas. 2006. *Seed to Seed: The Secret Life of Plants*. London: Bloomsbury.

Harding, Sandra. 2008. *Sciences from Below: Feminisms, Postcolonialities, and Modernities*. Durham, NC: Duke University Press.

Harland, Tony. 2003. Vygotsky's Zone of Proximal Development and Problem-based Learning: Linking a theoretical concept with practice through action research. *Teaching in Higher Education*, vol. 8 no. 2, pp. 263–272.

Harris, E. Nigel. 2013. Small states: Higher education in the English-speaking Caribbean, pp. 308–324 in Deryck M. Schreuder (ed.), *Universities for a New World*. New Delhi: Sage and Association of Commonwealth Universities.

Harvard Business School. 2018. The HBS Case Method. Online at www.hbs.edu/mba/academic-experience/Pages/the-hbs-case-method.aspx, accessed 4 March 2018.

Hau'ofa, Epeli. 2008. *We Are the Ocean: Selected Works*. Honolulu, HI: University of Hawai'i Press.

Hernándes Bringas, Héctor Hiram, Jaime Martuscelli Quintan, David Moctezuma Navarro, Humberto Muñoz García and José Narro Robles. 2015. Los desafios de las universidades de América Latina y el Caribe. ¿Qué somos y a dónde vamos? *Perfiles educativos*, vol. 37 no. 147, pp. 202–218.

Higher Education Council, National Board of Employment, Education and Training, Australia. 1996. *Equality, Diversity and Excellence: Advancing the National Higher Education Equity Framework*. Canberra: Australian Government Printing Service.

Hil, Richard. 2015. *Selling Students Short: Why You Won't Get the University Education You Deserve*. Sydney: Allen & Unwin.

Hinkson, John, Paul James, Alison Caddick, Simon Cooper, Melinda Hinkson and Dan Tout (eds). 2016. *Cold War to Hot Planet: Fifty Years of Arena*. Melbourne: Arena.

Hobson, John A. 2004. *The Eastern Origins of Western Civilization.* Cambridge: Cambridge University Press.

Holland, Dorothy C. and Margaret A. Eisenhart. 1990. *Educated in Romance: Women, Achievement, and College Culture.* Chicago, IL: University of Chicago Press.

Holloway, David. 1996. *Stalin and the Bomb: The Soviet Union and Nuclear Energy, 1939–1956.* New Haven, CT: Yale University Press.

Holmes, David R. 1989. *Stalking the Academic Communist: Intellectual Freedom and the Firing of Alex Novikoff.* Hanover, NH: University Press of New England.

Holmwood, John, Tom Hickey, Rachel Cohen and Sean Wallis (eds). 2016. *In Defence of Public Higher Education: Knowledge for a Successful Society.* UK Convention for Higher Education May 2016.

Hountondji, Paulin J. 1973. *Libertés: Contribution à la révolution Dahoméenne.* Cotonou: Éditions Renaissance.

Hountondji, Paulin J. (ed.). 1997. *Endogenous Knowledge: Research Trails.* Dakar: CODESRIA.

Hountondji, Paulin J. 2002. *The Struggle for Meaning: Reflections on Philosophy, Culture, and Democracy in Africa.* Athens, OH: Ohio University Press.

Hourani, Albert. 1991. *A History of the Arab Peoples.* New York: MJF Books.

Hudson, Liam. 1972. *The Cult of the Fact.* London: Jonathan Cape.

Hutchins, Robert Maynard. 1936. *The Higher Learning in America.* New Haven, CT: Yale University Press.

ICEF Monitor. 2016. MOOC enrolment surpassed 35 million in 2015. ICEF Monitor, 5 January 2016. http://monitor.icef.com/2016/01/mooc-enrolment-surpassed-35-million-in-2015/, accessed February 2018.

Ishikawa, Mayumi. 2012. University rankings, global models, and emerging hegemony: Critical analysis from Japan, pp. 81–99 in Brian Pusser, Ken Kemper, Simon Marginson and Imanol Ordorika (eds), *Universities and the Public Sphere: Knowledge Creation and State Building in the Era of Globalization.* New York: Routledge.

Ivancheva, Mariya. 2013. The Bolivarian University of Venezuela: A radical alternative in the global field of higher education? *Learning and Teaching*, vol. 6 no. 1, pp. 3–25.

Jansen, Jonathan. 2017. *As by Fire: The End of the South African University.* Cape Town: Tafelberg.

Jayaram, N. 2011. Sociology in Karnataka: The formation and decline of a discipline, pp. 188–210 in Sujata Patel (ed.), *Doing Sociology in India: Genealogies, Locations, and Practices.* New Delhi: Oxford University Press.

Jha, Narmadeshwar. 1994. Rabindranath Tagore (1861–1941). *Prospects: The Quarterly Review of Education (UNESCO)*, vol. 24 no. 3/4, pp. 603–619.

Jian Liu. 2012. Examining massification policies and their consequences for equality in Chinese higher education: A cultural perspective. *Higher Education*, vol. 64 no. 5, pp. 647–660.

Johnson, George M. 1966. The University of Nigeria, pp. 87–104 in Murray G. Ross (ed.), *New Universities in the Modern World*. London: Macmillan.

Johnson, Lesley (ed.). 1969. *Free U, Number 1. Sources, articles and documents on the free university*. Sydney: Free University.

Kagamé, Alexis (Abbé). 1956. *La Philosophie bantu-rwandaise de l'Être*. Brussels: Académie royale des sciences coloniales.

Kamin, Leon J. 1974. *The Science and Politics of I.Q.* Potomac, MD: Lawrence Erlbaum Associates.

Kartini. 2014. *The Complete Writings 1898–1904*. Ed. and trans. Joost Coté. Melbourne: Monash University Publishing.

Kenway, Jane and Johanna Fahey. 2009. *Globalizing the Research Imagination*. London: Routledge.

Kenway, Jane, Rebecca Boden and Johanna Fahey. 2015. Seeking the necessary 'resources of hope' in the neoliberal university, pp. 259–281 in Margaret Thornton (ed.), *Through a Glass Darkly: The Social Sciences Look at the Neoliberal University*. Canberra: Australian National University Press.

Kenway, Jane, Johanna Fahey, Debbie Epstein, Aaron Koh, Cameron McCarthy and Fazal Rizvi. 2017. *Class Choreographies: Elite Schools and Globalization*. London: Palgrave Macmillan.

Kimber, Megan and Lisa C. Ehrich. 2015. Are Australia's universities in deficit? A tale of generic managers, audit culture and casualization. *Journal of Higher Education Policy and Management*, vol. 37 no. 1, pp. 83–97.

Kippax, Susan, Raewyn Connell, Gary Dowsett and June Crawford. 1993. *Sustaining Safe Sex: Gay Communities Respond to AIDS*. London: Falmer Press.

Kishwar, Madhu and Ruth Vanita (ed.). 1984. *In Search of Answers: Indian Women's Voices from Manushi*. London: Zed Books.

Kniest, Paul. 2014. Do marketing slogans assist choice of university? *The Advocate (NTEU)*, vol. 21 no. 1, pp. 34–35.

Konrád, George and Ivan Szelényi. 1979. *The Intellectuals on the Road to Class Power*. Brighton: Harvester Press.

Kosík, Karel. 1976 [1961]. *Dialectics of the Concrete: A Study on Problems of Men and the World*. Dordrecht: Reidel.

Krishna, V. V. and Swapan Kumar Patra. 2016. Research and innovation in universities in India, pp. 163–189 in N. V. Varghese and Gorima Malik (eds), *India Higher Education Report 2015*. London: Routledge.

Krücken, Georg, Albrecht Blümel and Katharina Kloke. 2013. The managerial turn in higher education? On the interplay of organizational and occupational change in German academia. *Minerva*, vol. 51 no. 4, pp. 417–442.

Kuhn, Thomas S. 1970 [1962]. *The Structure of Scientific Revolutions*. 2nd edition. Chicago, IL: University of Chicago Press.

Kumar, Satendra. 2013. How Indian universities become profit machines. *Global Dialogue* (International Sociological Association), vol. 3 no. 3, at www.globaldialogue.isa-sociology.org.

Kwiek, Marek. 2014. From system expansion to system contraction: Access to higher education in Poland, pp. 193–215 in Anna Mountford-Zimdars, Daniel Sabbagh and David Post (eds), *Fair Access to Higher Education: Global Perspectives*. Chicago, IL: University of Chicago Press.

Lal, Vinay. 2002. *Empire of Knowledge: Culture and Plurality in the Global Economy*. London: Pluto.

Lamont, Michèle. 2009. *How Professors Think: Inside the Curious World of Academic Judgment*. Cambridge, MA: Harvard University Press.

Larivière, Vincent, Stefanie Haustein and Philippe Mongeon. 2015. The oligopoly of academic publishers in the digital era. *PLOS One*, vol. 10 no. 6. Online at https://doi.org/10.1371/journal.pone.0127502.

Larkins, Frank P. 2012. Trends in non-academic staff for Australian universities 2000 to 2010. L. H. Martin Institute *Insights* blog, at www.lhmartininstitute.edu.au/insights-blog.

Latour, Bruno. 2004. Why has critique run out of steam? From matters of fact to matters of concern. *Critical Inquiry*, no. 30, pp. 225–248.

Lawless, Ann. 2017. Affirming humanity: A case study of the activism of general/professional staff in the academy. *Australian Universities Review*, vol. 59 no. 2, pp. 50–58.

Le Guin, Ursula. 1974. *The Dispossessed*. London: Gollancz.

Lem, Stanislaw. 1970 [1961]. *Solaris*. London: Faber & Faber.

Lichtman, Jane. 1973. *Bring Your Own Bag: A Report on Free Universities*. Washington, DC: American Association for Higher Education.

Lillis, Theresa and Mary Jane Curry. 2010. *Academic Writing in a Global Context: The Politics and Practices of Publishing in English*. London: Routledge.

Lindqvist, Sven. 1978. *Gräv där du står* (Dig Where You Stand). Stockholm: Bonniers Grafiska.

Little, Graham. 1970. *The University Experience: An Australian Study.* Melbourne: Melbourne University Press.

Lopes Cardozo, Mieke T. A. 2012. Transforming pre-service teacher education in Bolivia: From indigenous denial to decolonisation? *Compare: A Journal of Comparative and International Education*, vol. 42 no. 5, pp. 751–772.

Lorenz, Chris. 2012. If you're so smart, why are you under surveillance? Universities, neoliberalism, and new public management. *Critical Inquiry*, vol. 38 no. 3, pp. 599–629.

Luckett, Kathy. 2016. Curriculum contestation in a post-colonial context: A view from the South. *Teaching in Higher Education*, vol. 21 no. 4, pp. 415–428.

Lugones, Maria. 2010. Toward a decolonial feminism. *Hypatia*, no. 25, pp. 742–759.

Lukács, Georg. 1971 [1923]. *History and Class Consciousness.* London: Merlin Press.

Lundh, A., S. Sismondo, J. Lexchin, O. A. Busuioc and L. Bero. 2012. Industry sponsorship and research outcome. *Cochrane Database of Systematic Reviews*, 12 December: MR000033. DOI: 10.1002/14651858.MR000033.pub2.

Lynch, Kathleen. 2015. Control by numbers: New managerialism and ranking in higher education. *Critical Studies in Education*, vol. 56 no. 2, pp. 190–207.

Macintyre, Stuart, André Brett and Gwilym Croucher. 2017. *No End of a Lesson: Australia's Unified National System of Higher Education.* Melbourne: Melbourne University Press.

Madrid, Sebastián. 2016. Diversidad sin diversidad: Los colegios particulares pagados de elite y la formación de la clase dominante en una sociedad de mercado, pp. 269–299 in J. Corvalán, A. Carrasco and J. E. García-Huidobro (eds), *La organización de mercado del sistema escolar chileno: Libertad, diversidad y desigualdad.* Santiago: Ediciones Universidad Católica.

Mama, Amina and Tessa Barnes (eds). 2007. Rethinking universities I and II. *Feminist Africa*, nos. 8 and 9.

Mamdani, Mahmood. 2009. *Scholars in the Marketplace: The Dilemmas of Neo-liberal Reform at Makerere University 1989–2005.* Cape Town: HSRC Press.

Marginson, Simon. 2006. Dynamics of national and global competition in higher education. *Higher Education*, vol. 52 no. 1, pp. 1–39.

Marginson, Simon. 2016. The worldwide trend to high participation higher education: Dynamics of social stratification in inclusive systems. *Higher Education*, vol. 72, pp. 413–434.

Matasar, Richard. 1996. A commercialist manifesto: Entrepreneurs, academics, and purity of the heart and soul. *Florida Law Review*, vol. 48, pp. 781–810. Online at http://heinonline.org/HOL/LandingPage?handle=hein.journals/uflr48&div=44&id=&page=.

Mathematical Review and Zentralblatt für Mathematik, MSC2010. Online at www.ams.org/mathscinet/msc/pdfs/classifications2010.pdf, accessed 15 March 2017.

Mattelart, Armand. 2003. *The Information Society: An Introduction.* London: Sage.

May, Robyn, David Peetz and Glenda Strahan. 2013. The casual academic workforce and labour market segmentation in Australia. *Labour and Industry*, vol. 23 no. 3, pp. 258–275.

Mazrui, Ali A. 1975. The African university as a multinational corporation: Problems of penetration and dependency. *Harvard Educational Review*, vol. 45 no. 2, pp. 191–210.

Mbembe, Achille Joseph. 2016. Decolonizing the university: New directions. *Arts and Humanities in Higher Education*, vol. 15 no. 1, pp. 29–45.

McCalman, Iain. 2009. *Darwin's Armada.* London: Simon & Schuster.

McCowan, Tristan. 2012. Is there a universal right to higher education? *British Journal of Educational Studies*, vol. 60 no. 2, pp. 111–128.

McCowan, Tristan. 2016. Forging radical alternatives in higher education: The case of Brazil. *Other Education: The Journal of Radical Alternatives*, vol. 5 no. 2, pp. 196–220.

McGettigan, Andrew. 2015. *The Treasury View of HE: Variable Human Capital Investment.* Political Research Papers Series, No. 6. London: Goldsmiths College, University of London.

McPhee, Peter. 2014. The Commonwealth used to fund universities: What happened? *The Conversation*, 12 June 2014. Online at https://theconversation.com/the-commonwealth-used-to-fund-universities-what-happened-27436, accessed 18 April 2018.

Melgarejo, Patricia Medina (ed.). 2015. *Pedagogías insumisas: Movimientos político-pedagógicos y memorias colectivas de educaciones otras en América Latina.* Mexico: Juan Pablos.

Mistral, Gabriela. 2010. *Antología: Gabriela Mistral en verso y prosa.* Lima: Academia española and Asociación de academias de lengua española.

Mkandawire, Thandika. 2000. Non-organic intellectuals and 'learning' in policy-making Africa. Paper for EGDI seminar *What Do Aid Agencies and Their Co-operating Partners Learn from Their Experiences?*, 24 August 2000.

Mkandawire, Thandika (ed.). 2005. *African Intellectuals: Rethinking Politics, Language, Gender and Development.* Dakar: CODESRIA Books and London: Zed Books.

Mönckeberg, María Olivia. 2013. *Con fines de lucro: La escandalosa historia de las universidades privadas en Chile.* Santiago: Penguin Random House.

Morgan, George and Julian Wood. 2017. The 'academic career' in the era of flexploitation, pp. 82–97 in Emiliana Armano, Arianna Bore and Annalisa Murgia (eds), *Mapping Precariousness, Labour Insecurity and Uncertain Livelihoods: Subjectivities and Resistance.* London: Routledge.

Morrish, Liz and The Analogue University Writing Collective. 2017. Academic identities in the managed university: Neoliberalism and resistance at Newcastle University, UK. *Australian Universities Review*, vol. 59 no. 2, pp. 23–35.

Morrison, Heather. 2015. Open Access to scholarly knowledge: The new commons, pp. 256–266 in Patricia W. Elliot and Daryl H. Hepting (eds), *Free Knowledge.* Regina: University of Regina Press.

Mountz, Alison and ten others. 2015. For slow scholarship: A feminist politics of resistance through collective action in the neoliberal university. *ACME: International E-Journal for Critical Geographies*, vol. 14 no. 4, pp. 1235–1259.

Muhr, Thomas. 2010. Counter-hegemonic regionalism and higher education for all: Venezuela and the ALBA. *Globalisation, Societies and Education*, vol. 8 no. 1, pp. 39–57.

Muhr, Thomas. 2016. Equity of access to higher education in the context of South–South cooperation in Latin America: A pluri-scalar analysis. *Higher Education*, vol. 72, pp. 557–571.

Münch, Richard. 2014. *Academic Capitalism: Universities in the Global Struggle for Excellence.* New York: Routledge.

Naidoo, Rajani. 2016. The competition fetish in higher education: Varieties, animators and consequences. *British Journal of Sociology of Education*, vol. 37 no. 1, pp. 1–10.

Nanda, Meera. 2016. *Science in Saffron: Skeptical Essays on History of Science.* Gurgaon: Three Essays Collective.

National Alliance for Public Universities. 2014. *A Charter for Australia's Public Universities.* Online at https://napuaustralia.org/charter/, accessed 10 April 2018.

Needham, Joseph. 1954. *Science and Civilisation in China*, vol. 1. Cambridge: Cambridge University Press.

Newman, John Henry. 1873 [1852]. *The Idea of a University: Defined and Illustrated.* London: Basil Montagu Pickering.

Nobel, Alfred Bernhard. 1895. Will. English translation at www.nobelprize.org/alfred_nobel/will/will-full.html, accessed 25 June 2017.

Norris, Ray. 2017. Exoplanet discovery by an amateur astronomer shows the power of citizen science. *The Conversation*, 7 April 2017. Online at https://theconversation.com/exoplanet-discovery-by-an-amateur-astronomer-shows-the-power-of-citizen-science-75912.

NTEU Sydney University Branch. 2015. *University of Sydney 2014–15: A Counter-report. How the University Is and How It Could Be.* Sydney: National Tertiary Education Union.

O'Nolan, Brian [aka Flann O'Brien, Myles na Gopaleen]. 2007. *The Best of Myles: A Selection from 'Cruiskeen Lawn'.* London: Harper Perennial.

Odora Hoppers, Catherine A. (ed.). 2002. *Indigenous Knowledge and the Integration of Knowledge Systems: Towards a Philosophy of Articulation.* Claremont: New Africa Books.

Oldfield, Sophie. 2015. Between activism and the academy: The urban as political terrain. *Urban Studies*, vol. 52 no. 11, pp. 2072–2086.

Parker, Lee. 2011. University corporatisation: Driving redefinition. *Critical Perspectives on Accounting*, vol. 22, pp. 434–450.

Parker, Martin. 2014. University, Ltd: Changing a business school. *Organization*, vol. 21 no. 2, pp. 281–292.

Parkin, Frank. 1979. *Marxism and Class Theory: A Bourgeois Critique.* London: Tavistock.

Pashler, Harold and Eric-Jan Wagenmakers. 2012. Editors' introduction to the special section on replicability in psychological science: A crisis of confidence? *Perspectives on Psychological Science*, vol. 7 no. 6, pp. 528–530.

Pearson, Karl. 1937. *The Grammar of Science.* London: Dent.

Peetz, David, Glenda Strachan and Carolyn Troup. 2014. Discipline, change and gender in the academic workforce. Paper for the 28th conference of the Association of Industrial Relations Academics of Australia and New Zealand, 2014.

Pellew, Jill. 2014. 'Utopian' universities: A 50-year retrospective. *Past and Future: The Magazine of the Institute of Historical Research*, no. 15, pp. 10–11.

Peters, Michael A. 2015. Why is my curriculum White? *Educational Philosophy and Theory*, vol. 47 no. 7, pp. 641–646.

Pick, David, Stephen Teo and Melissa Yeung. 2012. Friend or foe? New managerialism and technical, administrative and clerical support staff in Australian universities. *Higher Education Quarterly*, vol. 66 no. 1, pp. 3–23.

Pickering, Andrew. 1995. *The Mangle of Practice: Time, Agency, and Science.* Chicago, IL: University of Chicago Press.

Pietsch, Tamson. 2013. *Empire of Scholars: Universities, Networks and the British Academic World 1850–1939*. Manchester: Manchester University Press.

Popper, Karl R. 1959 [1934]. *The Logic of Scientific Discovery*. New York: Harper and Row.

Powell, Walter W. and Jason Owen-Smith. 2002. The new world of knowledge production in the life sciences, pp. 107–130 in Steven Brint (ed.), *The Future of the City of Intellect: The Changing American University*. Stanford, CA: Stanford University Press.

Power, Michael. 1999. *The Audit Society*. 2nd edition. Oxford: Oxford University Press.

Precarias a la deriva. 2018 [2002]. Adrift through the circuits of feminized precarious work. Online at eipcp.net/transversal/0704/precarias1/en, accessed 1 August 2018.

Probert, Belinda. 2005. 'I just don't fit in': Gender and unequal outcomes in academic careers. *Gender, Work and Organization*, vol. 12 no. 1, pp. 50–72.

Pszenicki, Chris. 1979. The Flying University. *Index on Censorship*, no. 6, pp. 19–22.

Pulido, Laura. 2014. Faculty governance at the University of Southern California, pp. 145–168 in Priya Chatterjee and Sunaina Maira (eds), *The Imperial University*. Minneapolis, MN: University of Minnesota Press.

Qi, Xiaoying. 2015. Globalized higher education, pp. 328–343 in Bryan S. Turner and Robert J. Holton (eds), *Routledge International Handbook of Globalization Studies*. 2nd edition. London: Routledge.

Radice, Hugo. 2013. How we got here: UK higher education under neoliberalism. *ACME: An International Journal for Critical Geographies*, vol. 12 no. 2, pp. 407–418.

Raffe, David. 1977. Social class and entry to further education. *Scottish Education Studies*, vol. 9 no. 2, pp. 100–111.

Raju, Suvrat, Prajval Shastri and Ravinder Banyal. 2017. *A Fact-Finding Report on the Events at the University of Hyderabad*. Self-published 2 January 2017.

Rama, Claudio. 2012. El negocio universitario 'for-profit' en América Latina. *Revista de la educación superior*, vol. 41 no. 164, pp. 59–95.

Readings, Bill. 1996. *The University in Ruins*. Cambridge, MA: Harvard University Press.

Reed, Conor Tomás. 2013. 'Treasures that prevail': Adrienne Rich, the SEEK program, and social movements at the City College of New York, 1968–1972, pp. 36–65 in Iemanja Brown and seven others (eds), *'What We Are Part Of': Teaching at CUNY: 1968–1974*.

Lost and Found, series 4, number 3, part 2. New York: The CUNY Poetics Document Initiative.

Reuben, Julie A. 1996. *The Making of the Modern University: Intellectual Transformation and the Marginalization of Morality*. Chicago, IL: University of Chicago Press.

Rhoads, Robert A., Xioayang Wang, Xiaoguang Shi and Yongcai Chang. 2014. *China's Rising Research Universities: A New Era of Global Ambition*. Baltimore, MD: Johns Hopkins University Press.

Richards, Paul. 2016. *Ebola: How a People's Science Helped End an Epidemic*. London: Zed Books.

Roberts, Celia and Raewyn Connell (eds). 2016. *Southern Feminisms*. Special issue of *Feminist Theory*, vol. 17 no. 2.

Robertson, Susan L. and Kris Olds. 2017. Rankings as global (monetising) scopic systems, pp. 54–76 in Ellen Hazelkorn (ed.), *Global Rankings and the Geopolitics of Higher Education*. London: Routledge.

Robinson, Andrew. 2002. *The Man Who Deciphered Linear B: The Story of Michael Ventris*. London: Thames & Hudson.

Robinson, Maureen and Dirk Meerkotter. 2003. Fifteen years of action research for political and educational emancipation at a South African university. *Educational Action Research*, vol. 11 no. 3, pp. 447–465.

Romilly, Jacqueline de. 2012 [1956]. *The Mind of Thucydides*. Ithaca, NY: Cornell University Press.

Rorty, Richard and Pascal Engel. 2007. *What's the Use of Truth?* New York: Columbia University Press.

Rosenberg, Rosalind. 1982. *Beyond Separate Spheres: Intellectual Roots of Modern Feminism*. New Haven, CT: Yale University Press.

Ross, Andrew. 2009. The rise of the global university, pp. 18–31 in Edu-factory Collective, *Toward a Global Autonomous University*. New York: Autonomedia.

Ross, Murray G. (ed.). 1966. *New Universities in the Modern World*. London: Macmillan.

Rothengatter, Maarten and Richard Hil. 2013. A precarious presence: Some realities and challenges of academic casualization in Australian universities. *Australian Universities Review*, vol. 55 no. 2, pp. 51–59.

RUIICAY [Red de universidades indigenas, interculturales, comunitarias de Abya Yala]. 2012. *Educación superior y pueblos indígenas*. January. Online at http://ruiicay.uraccan.edu.ni/, accessed 14 February 2018.

Sánchez Lopera, Alejandro and Rocío Rueda Ortiz. 2014. María Cristina Laverde Toscano: La artesanía de una práctica investigativa para las sciencias sociales. *Nomadas*, no. 40, pp. 13–33.

Santelices, Maria Veronica and Mark Wilson. 2010. Unfair treatment? The case of Freedle, the SAT, and the standardization approach to differential item functioning. *Harvard Educational Review*, vol. 80 no. 1, pp. 106–134.

Santos, Boaventura de Sousa. 2014. *Epistemologies of the South: Justice against Epistemicide*. Boulder, CO: Paradigm Publishers.

Santos Herceg, José. 2006. La Universidad chilena hoy: El espejismo de su progreso. *Estudios avanzados interactivas*, vol. 5 no. 7. Online at http://web.usach.cl/nevistaidea/.

Schiebinger, Londa and Claudia Swan (ed.). 2005. *Colonial Botany: Science, Commerce, and Politics in the Early Modern World*. Philadelphia, PA: University of Pennsylvania Press.

Schwartz, Joseph M. 2014. Resisting the exploitation of contingent faculty labor in the neoliberal university: The challenge of building solidarity between tenured and non-tenured faculty. *New Political Science*, vol. 36 no. 4, pp. 504–522.

Sebalt, Darlene, Allyson Holbrook and Sid Bourke. 2012. The rise of 'professional staff' and demise of the 'non-academic': A study of university staffing nomenclature preferences. *Journal of Higher Education Policy and Management*, vol. 34 no. 5, pp. 463–472.

Secretaría de Igualdad del CIEG-UNAM. 2018. Presencia de mujeres y hombres en la UNAM: Una radiografia. Online at www.tendencias.cieg.unam.mx/radigrafia.html, accessed 16 February 2018.

Selkirk, David R. and Frank J. Burrows (eds). 1987. *Confronting Creationism: Defending Darwin*. Sydney: New South Wales University Press.

Shahjahan, Riyad A. and Clara Morgan. 2016. Global competition, coloniality, and the geopolitics of knowledge in higher education. *British Journal of Sociology of Education*, vol. 37 no. 1, pp. 92–109.

Shapin, Steven. 1994. *A Social History of Truth: Civility and Science in Seventeenth-century England*. Chicago, IL: University of Chicago Press.

Shariati, Ali. 1981. *Man and Islam*. Houston, TX: Free Islamic Literature.

Shariati, Ali. 1986. What is to be done: A practical plan for Husayniah Irshad, pp. 103–160 in *What Is To Be Done: The Enlightened Thinkers and an Islamic Renaissance*. Houston, TX: The Institute for Research and Islamic Studies.

Sharma, G. D. 2016. Diversification of higher education in India, pp. 199–227 in N. V. Varghese and Malik Garima, *India Higher Education Report 2015*. London: Routledge.

Sharp, Geoff, and Doug White. 1968. Features of the intellectually trained. *Arena*, no. 15, pp. 30–33.

Shay, Suellen and Tai Peseta. 2016. A socially just curriculum reform agenda. *Teaching in Higher Education*, vol. 21 no. 4, pp. 361–366.

Slaughter, Sheila and Larry L. Leslie. 1997. *Academic Capitalism: Politics, Policies, and the Entrepreneurial University*. Baltimore, MD: Johns Hopkins University Press.

Smith, Adam. 1910 [1776]. *The Wealth of Nations*. London: Dent.

Smith, Linda Tuhiwai. 1997. Decolonising intellectual identity: Māori/woman/academic, pp. 182–210 in Michael Peters (ed.), *Cultural Politics and the University in Aotearoa/New Zealand*, Palmerston North: Dunmore Press.

Smith, Linda Tuhiwai. 1999. *Decolonizing Methodologies: Research and Indigenous Peoples*. London and New York: Zed Press and Dunedin: University of Otago Press.

Smith, Richard. 2012. University futures. *Journal of Philosophy of Education*, vol. 46 no. 4, pp. 649–662.

Somerville, Margaret and Tony Perkins. 2010. *Singing the Coast*. Canberra: Aboriginal Studies Press.

Sonnenberg, Laura. 2017. The highest-paid public university presidents. *Forbes*, 17 July 2017. Online at www.forbes.com/sites/laurensonnenberg/2017/07/17/the-top-paid-public-university-presidents/#13e624c2114c, accessed 15 April 2018.

Srigley, Don. 2015. Dear parents: Everything you need to know about your son and daughter's university but don't. *LA Review of Books*, 9 December 2015. Online at https://lareviewofbooks.org/article/dear-parents-everything-you-need-to-know-about-your-son-and-daughters-university-but-dont/, accessed 10 April 2018.

Stacey, Judith. 2011. *Unhitched: Love, Marriage and Family Values from West Hollywood to Western China*. New York: New York University Press.

Steinmetz, George (ed.). 2013. *Sociology and Empire: The Imperial Entanglements of a Discipline*. Durham, NC: Duke University Press.

Stroebe, Wolfgang, Tom Postmes and Russell Spears. 2012. Scientific misconduct and the myth of self-correction in science. *Perspectives on Psychological Science*, vol. 7 no. 6, pp. 670–688.

Sturm, Sean and Stephen Turner. 2011. The idea of the university. *Arena Magazine*, no. 111, pp. 16–19.

Subramaniam, Mangala, Robert Perrucci and David Whitlock. 2012. Intellectual closure: A theoretical framework linking knowledge, power, and the corporate university. *Critical Sociology*, vol. 40 no. 3, pp. 411–430.

Sweet, Paul R. 1980. *Wilhelm von Humboldt: A Biography*, vol. 2. Columbus, OH: Ohio State University Press.

Symes, Colin. 1996. Selling futures: A new image for Australian universities? *Studies in Higher Education*, vol. 21 no. 2, pp. 133–147.

Szekeres, Judy. 2011. Professional staff carve out a new space. *Journal of Higher Education Policy and Management*, vol. 33 no. 6, pp. 679–691.

Tancred-Sheriff, Peta. 1985. Craft, hierarchy and bureaucracy: Modes of control of the academic labour process. *Canadian Journal of Sociology*, vol. 10 no. 4, pp. 369–390.

Tarski, Alfred. 1956 [1931]. The concept of truth in formalized languages, pp. 152–278 in *Logic, Semantics, Metamathematics*. Oxford: Oxford University Press.

Tharu, Susie. 2016. The promise and lie of the university. Commentary online at www.tehelka.com/2016/02/the-promise-and-the-lie-of-the-university/, accessed 11 April 2018.

The Times Higher. 2005. World university rankings: The top 200. *Times Higher Education Supplement*, 28 October 2005.

Thornton, Margaret. 2012. *Privatising the Public University: The Case of Law*. Abingdon: Routledge.

Thornton, Margaret (ed.). 2015. *Through a Glass Darkly: The Social Sciences Look at the Neoliberal University*. Canberra: Australian National University Press.

Thrift, Nigel. 2016. Universities 2035. *Perspectives: Policy and Practice in Higher Education*, vol. 20 no. 1, pp. 12–16.

Tierney, Robert and Wei Kan. 2016. Knowledge globalization within and across the People's Republic of China and the United States: A cross-national study of internationalization of educational research in the early 21st century. *American Educational Research Journal*, vol. 53 no. 6, pp. 1759–1791.

Tierney, William G. and Guilbert C. Hentschke. 2007. *New Players, Different Game: Understanding the Rise of For-Profit Colleges and Universities*. Baltimore, MD: Johns Hopkins University Press.

Treanor, Brian. 2006. Slow university: A manifesto. Online at http://faculty.lmu.edu/briantreanor/slow-university-a-manifesto/, accessed 9 October 2017.

Trumpbour, John (ed.). 1989. *How Harvard Rules: Reason in the Service of Empire*. Boston, MA: South End Press.

Tuchman, Gaye. 2009. *Wannabe U: Inside the Corporate University*. Chicago, IL: University of Chicago Press.

Turney, Clifford, Ursula Bygott and Peter Chippendale. 1991. *Australia's First: A History of the University of Sydney*, vol. 1: 1850–1939. Sydney: Hale & Iremonger.

Tytherleigh, M. Y., C. Webb, C. L. Cooper and C. Ricketts. 2005. Occupational stress in UK higher education institutes: A comparative study of all staff categories. *Higher Education Research and Development*, vol. 24 no. 1, pp. 41–61.

UN General Assembly resolution 68/165, *Right to the Truth*, A/RES/68/165 (18 December 2013). Online at undocs.org/A/RES/68/165.

UNESCO Global Education Policy Report. 2017. *Policy Paper 30: Six Ways to Ensure Higher Education Leaves No One Behind.* Paris: UNESCO.

United Nations. *Statistical Yearbook 2017*. Online at https://unstats.un.org/unsd/publications/statistical-yearbook/, accessed 27 February 2018.

Universities Australia. 2015. *2014 Selected Inter-institutional Gender Equity Statistics.* Canberra: Universities Australia.

University of Cape Town. 2015. UCT abolishes outsourcing. *UCT Daily News*, 29 October 2015. Online at www.uct.za/dailynews/id=9439.

University of Córdoba Students Federation, Directive Commission. 1918. *From the Argentinian Youth of Córdoba to the Free Men of South America* [the 'Liminar Manifesto' or 'Córdoba Declaration']. English translation online at https://en.wikisource.org/wiki/Translation:Liminar_Manifesto.

Usher, Alex. 2017. A short global history of rankings, pp. 23–53 in Ellen Hazelkorn (ed.), *Global Rankings and the Geopolitics of Higher Education.* London: Routledge.

Välimaa, Jussi. 2012. The corporatization of National Universities in Finland, pp. 101–119 in Brian Pusser, Ken Kemper, Simon Marginson and Imanol Ordorika (eds), *Universities and the Public Sphere: Knowledge Creation and State Building in the Era of Globalization.* New York: Routledge.

Van der Veer, René and Jaan Valsiner. 1991. *Understanding Vygotsky: A Quest for Synthesis.* Oxford: Blackwell.

Veblen, Thorstein. 1959 [1918]. *The Higher Learning in America: A Memorandum on the Conduct of Universities by Business Men.* New York: Sagamore Press.

Vessuri, H. 2003. Science, politics, and democratic participation in policy-making: A Latin American view. *Technology in Society*, vol. 25, pp. 263–273.

Vidya Ashram. 2009. The global autonomous university, pp. 165–170 in Edu-factory Collective, *Toward a Global Autonomous University.* New York: Autonomedia.

wa Thiong'o, Ngũgĩ. 1986. *Decolonizing the Mind: The Politics of Language in African Literature.* London: James Currey.

wa Thiong'o, Ngũgĩ. 1993. *Moving the Centre: The Struggle for Cultural Freedoms*. London: James Currey.

Wace, N. 1977. Assessment of dispersal of plant species: The car-borne flora in Canberra. *Proceedings of the Ecological Society of Australia*, vol. 10, pp. 167–186.

Wadsworth, Yoland. 1984. *Do It Yourself Social Research*. Melbourne: Victorian Council of Social Service.

Wajcman, Judy. 1998. *Managing Like a Man: Women and Men in Corporate Management*. Cambridge: Polity.

Walker, Shayne, Anaru Eketone and Anita Gibbs. 2006. An exploration of Kaupapa Māori research, its principles, processes and applications. *International Journal of Social Research Methodology*, vol. 9 no. 4, pp. 331–344.

Wankhede, Govardhan. 2016. Perspectives on social group disparities in higher education, pp. 97–112 in N. V. Varghese and Malik Garima, *India Higher Education Report 2015*. London: Routledge.

Ward, Steven C. 2012. *Neoliberalism and the Global Restructuring of Knowledge and Education*. New York: Routledge.

Ware, Mark and Michael Mabe. 2015. *The STM Report: An Overview of Scientific and Scholarly Journal Publishing*. 4th edition. The Hague: International Association of Scientific, Technical and Medical Publishers.

Warner, Marina. 2015. Learning my lesson. *London Review of Books*, 19 March. Online at www.lrb.co.uk/v37/no6/marina-warner/learning-my-lesson, accessed 18 April 2018.

Watts, Rob. 2017. *Public Universities, Managerialism and the Value of Higher Education*. London: Palgrave Macmillan.

Welch, Anthony (ed.). 2005. *The Professoriate: Profile of a Profession*. Dordrecht: Springer.

Welch, Anthony. 2016. Audit culture and academic production: Re-shaping Australian social science research output 1993–2013. *Higher Education Policy*, vol. 29 no. 4, pp. 511–538.

Welch, Anthony. 2017. Higher education and the developmental state: The view from East and South East Asia, pp. 359–387 in Toby Carroll and Darryl S. L. Jarvis (eds), *Asia after the Developmental State: Disembedding Autonomy*. Cambridge: Cambridge University Press.

Whitchurch, Celia. 2008. Shifting identities and blurring boundaries: The emergence of Thirdspace professionals in UK higher education. *Higher Education Quarterly*, vol. 62 no. 4, pp. 377–396.

Whittington, H. B. 1975. The enigmatic animal *Opabinia Regalis*, Middle Cambrian, Burgess Shale, British Columbia. *Philosophical*

Transactions of the Royal Society of London, Series B, Biological Sciences, vol. 271, no. 910.

Whitty, Geoff, Annette Hayton and Sarah Tang. 2015. Who you know, what you know and knowing the ropes: A review of evidence about access to higher education institutions in England. *Review of Education*, vol. 3 no. 1, pp. 27–67.

Williams, John. 2012 [1965]. *Stoner*. London: Vintage.

Williamson, Ben. 2018. The hidden architecture of higher education: Building a big data infrastructure for the 'smarter university'. *International Journal of Educational Technology in Higher Education*, vol. 15 no. 12.

Winchester, Hilary P. M. and Lynette Browning. 2015. Gender equality in academia: A critical reflection. *Journal of Higher Education Policy and Management*, vol. 37 no. 3, pp. 269–281.

Wolpman, Jim. 2017. Alive in the 60s: The Midpeninsula Free University. Online at www.midpeninsulafreeu.com, accessed 2 October 2017.

Wootton, David. 2016. *The Invention of Science: A New History of the Scientific Revolution*. London: Penguin.

World Academic Summit. 2018. *Website at* www.theworldsummitseries.com, accessed 13 February 2018.

World Bank. 2002. *Constructing Knowledge Societies: New Challenges for Tertiary Education*. Washington, DC: World Bank.

Xiang Biao. 2009. The social production of hierarchy and what we can do about it: Notes from Asia, pp. 80–83 in Edu-factory Collective, *Toward a Global Autonomous University*. New York: Autonomedia.

Younging, Gregory. 2015. *Gnaritas nullius* (no one's knowledge): The essence of traditional knowledge and its colonization through Western legal regimes, pp. 149–179 in Patricia W. Elliot and Daryl H. Hepting (eds), *Free Knowledge*. Regina: University of Regina Press.

Zeghal, Malika. 2007. The 'recentring' of religious knowledge and discourse: The case of al-Azhar in twentieth-century Egypt, pp. 107–130 in Robert W. Hefner and Muhammad Qasim Zaman (eds), *Schooling Islam: The Culture and Politics of Modern Muslim Education*. Princeton, NJ: Princeton University Press.

Zucker, Kenneth J. and Robert L. Spitzer. 2005. Was the Gender Identity Disorder of Childhood diagnosis introduced into DSM-III as a backdoor manoeuver to replace homosexuality? A historical note. *Journal of Sex and Mental Therapy*, vol. 31 no. 1, pp. 31–42.

Acknowledgements

Intellectual work is collective labour, and this book builds on the labour of hundreds of others, as indicated in the notes. I am particularly grateful to those who have helped in the making of this text, Kath Selkirk, Nour Dados and Monica Seini, and for the advice and support of Kylie Benton-Connell, Patricia Selkirk, Mignonne Breier, Patrick Brownlee, Fernando Serrano, Amy Johnston, Sebastián Madrid and Stephen Tomsen. I have drawn from research jointly done with João Maia, Robert Morrell, Fran Collyer, Patrick Brownlee, Rebecca Pearse, Julian Wood and the late June Crawford; my thanks to all members of these teams. I owe a wider debt to the many students, colleagues and friends from whom I have learnt during university struggles and reforms, especially fellow-members of the National Tertiary Education Union.

Index